9 LIFE SKILLS FOR TEENS TO SUCCEED

WIN AT SCHOOL, WORK, & LIFE

RAMAN KEANE

CONTENTS

INTRODUCTION

A fresh start is waiting for you, and it's a big one! You're about to begin your first job, head off to college, or take on a challenge you've been preparing for—and there's a world of excitement ahead.

But, let's be honest, there's a little bit of nervousness mixed in, too. After all, it's a new chapter, and that can be intimidating. You might be thinking, "Am I actually ready for this? Do I have the skills I need to handle what's coming next?"

If your answer is something like, "Uh...maybe?"—don't worry, you're definitely not alone. In fact, a survey conducted by YouScience found that a whopping 75% of high school graduates feel unprepared for making major life decisions related to careers and college (Hornbuckle, 2022). That's a pretty huge number of people stepping into adulthood with more uncertainty than they'd like to admit, especially when it comes to crucial life skills like time management, money handling, effective communication, and making big decisions!

But here's the thing—none of that is really your fault. These kinds of skills aren't exactly taught in school, and there's no formal class on navigating adulthood.

So, here you are, stepping into a whole new world with some excitement, some doubt, and maybe even a bit of fear. What if you don't have what it takes to succeed? What if you mess up?

We all get those feelings when stepping into the unknown. In fact, I've been there myself. Before my first full-time job, I remember feeling a mix of excitement and total panic. I was pumped to start this new chapter, but at the same time, I was thinking, "What if I fail?" What if I don't know what I'm doing?

Those "what ifs" can really start to pile up when you're about to take on something new.

Maybe you've felt that way, too. Maybe you've just started a new class, you're leading a group project for the first time, or you're about to dive into something totally unfamiliar, like starting your very first job.

Let me tell you, feeling underprepared is completely normal!

It's one of those universal experiences that so many of us face when trying something new. But here's the silver lining: with the right skills and the right support system, navigating the unknown becomes a lot easier and, yes—way less stressful.

Why This Book Exists

That's exactly why I wrote this book. I didn't write it to hand you all the answers (because, let's be real, life isn't about handing out answers on a silver platter). Instead, I wrote this book to give you the tools and skills you need to handle whatever life throws at you.

My goal is to help you build a skill set that makes your life smoother, your stress levels lower, and your overall experience way more fun. After all, adulting doesn't have to be as hard as it seems, and trust me, with the right knowledge and approach, it can actually be really rewarding!

So, what exactly will you get out of this book? Think of this book as your personal life skills survival guide. It's your toolkit for handling all those big moments and everyday challenges with confidence, creativity, and a little bit of flair. The skills you'll build in these pages are not just about surviving your new job or college; they're about thriving in any situation that comes your way. Whether you're making new friends, handling your finances, or dealing with the curveballs life throws at you, this book will give you the foundation to tackle it all with ease.

What You'll Learn

Let's dive into a sneak peek of what you'll learn throughout these chapters:

- **Emotional Intelligence:** Learn how to recognize and understand your own emotions, connect with others on a deeper level, and handle stress like a total pro. Emotions are tricky, but knowing how to manage them can make all the difference when it comes to your overall success and well-being.
- **Critical Thinking:** The key to good decision-making is asking the right questions and thinking things through before jumping into action. This chapter will

help you sharpen your critical thinking skills so you can make sound decisions, solve problems with ease, and feel confident in your choices.

- **Communication Skills:** Sending a quick text, delivering a presentation, or chatting with friends—all of these require effective communication skills. In this chapter, we'll focus on saying what you mean, getting heard, and, most importantly, becoming an active listener.

- **Using Technology Wisely:** Technology is everywhere, and when you learn how to use it to your advantage, it opens up so many possibilities. From staying organized with digital tools to creating new opportunities with tech, you'll discover how to harness the power of the digital world.

- **Handling Change & Challenges:** Life is unpredictable, and we can't always control what happens next. But we can control how we respond. This chapter will teach you how to adapt to new situations, bounce back from setbacks, and keep moving forward with a positive attitude.

- **Understanding Money:** Money doesn't have to be a mystery. From budgeting and saving to investing for your future, you'll learn how to manage your finances like a boss. This chapter will help you take control of your financial destiny so you can feel secure and confident in your money decisions.

- **Time Management:** Time is a limited resource, and figuring out how to manage it without getting overwhelmed is crucial. In this chapter, we'll explore techniques that help you prioritize your tasks, stay organized, and still make time for the things you love.

- **Building Strong Relationships**: Making new friends, keeping up with existing relationships, or networking for your career—all of these rely on strong relationship-building skills. You'll discover how to create meaningful connections and build a solid support system.
- **Creative Thinking and Problem-Solving:** Creativity isn't just about drawing or painting—it's about thinking outside the box and finding new solutions to everyday challenges. This chapter will help you tap into your creative potential and tackle problems in innovative ways.

Each chapter is packed with real-life examples, fun activities, and hands-on tips that make these skills easy to practice and develop. And don't worry—no need to master everything all at once.

Life is a journey, and this book is here to guide you, step-by-step, as you build your confidence and grow these essential skills over time. Starting a new job, heading off to college, or preparing for whatever life has in store?

This book will be your trusty companion as you navigate those early adult years with clarity, confidence, and a lot less stress.

Let's dive into your journey to success, one skill at a time!

Let's do this!

1

EMOTIONAL INTELLIGENCE (EQ)

 "Nobody cares how much you know until they know how much you care."

— THEODORE ROOSEVELT

Have you ever stepped into a room and felt the vibe right away? Maybe you noticed your friend was having a rough day even though they hadn't said anything, or you kept her cool during a heated discussion while everyone else got upset.

That's emotional intelligence—sometimes called EQ in action.

Emotional quotient is all about understanding your emotions and being aware of others' feelings. It's a skill that can help you communicate better, build stronger relationships, and handle life's ups and downs.

This chapter will discuss what EQ means, why it matters, and some practical ways to develop it.

What is Emotional Intelligence?

Emotional intelligence is your personal roadmap to handling emotions— yours and those around you.

It's about recognizing your feelings, understanding why you feel that way, and determining the best way to respond. It also means paying attention to the emotions of others so you can support them in the right way.

For instance, if you can tell a friend is *really* upset and you think you know how to help, you have the opportunity to build a stronger and more meaningful relationship. And that, my friends, is the power of the emotional quotient!

Psychologists Daniel Goleman and Peter Salovey were among the first to study emotional intelligence (EQ). Their research showed that EQ is just as important as academic intelligence because it can help you make smart choices, solve problems effectively, and create long-term and healthy relationships with the people in your life (Freedman, 2024).

Now, let's look closer.

This "roadmap" isn't just a simple set of directions. It's a complex, ever-evolving system. Think of it as a GPS that constantly recalibrates based on your internal and external environments. Recognizing your feelings isn't just about labeling them— "sad," "angry," "happy." It's about understanding the nuances, the subtle shifts in emotional terrain.

Why is that anger simmering or that sadness lingering? Is it a reaction to a specific event or a deeper, underlying issue?

Understanding "why" requires introspection and a willingness to look inward and confront uncomfortable truths. It's about tracing the roots of your emotions, identifying triggers, and recognizing patterns.

This isn't a passive process; it demands active engagement with your inner self. And then, there's the "best way to respond." This isn't about suppressing emotions or putting on a facade. It's about finding healthy, constructive outlets, whether it's through communication, creative expression, or simply taking a moment to breathe and reflect.

But EQ isn't just about managing your own internal world. It's about navigating the intricate web of life's interactions. It requires empathy, the ability to step into another person's shoes and understand their perspective. It's about listening not just to their words but to the unspoken emotions that lie beneath. And it's about offering support in a way that resonates with them, not just with what you think they need.

This skill is critical because healthy relationships are the cornerstone of a fulfilling life.

Why EQ Matters

- **Stronger Friendships**: When you understand how your friends and family feel, you can better support them.
- **Smarter decisions**: Awareness of your emotions helps you think before acting. This means you are in control

of your feelings and are much less likely to make rash decisions you could regret in the future.

- **Better leadership**: Great leaders don't just give orders but inspire and guide others using emotional intelligence.
- **Less stress**: Understanding your emotions helps you manage stress in a healthy way instead of letting it take over.

The Five Key Parts of EQ

1. Self-Awareness

What do we mean by self-awareness?

Self-awareness means knowing what you're feeling and why. It's like holding up a mirror to your emotional self so you can understand what's happening inside.

Think of it like this: Have you ever been in a rancid mood but couldn't quite figure out why or what triggered you to feel that way? Maybe it was a tough test at school or an argument with your parents. Perhaps it's as simple as you not getting enough sleep the night before.

When you can pinpoint the cause of the trigger, it's much easier to handle the emotions that come with it and redirect yourself toward your happy place.

It doesn't stop there! Self-awareness can also help you see how your emotions affect the people around you. When you understand where you are coming from and how you feel about that, you're a lot more likely to stay calm and communicate clearly.

Try this: Keep a small journal to jot down how you feel each day. What made you happy, stressed, or frustrated? What did you learn about yourself in that situation? What inspired those feelings? Over time, you'll start to notice patterns and better understand yourself and your role in the world around you.

2. Self-Control

Self-control sounds like a broad term, but it really means managing our emotions and reactions, especially when encountering something frustrating.

Picture this: you're waiting in line, and someone suddenly cuts in front of you. What's your first instinct?

Is it to snap at them?

Enter Self-control, the tool in our emotional toolbelt that allows us to take a step back, breathe, and decide on the best response.

Perhaps it's better to get their attention politely, or maybe it's better to let it go and avoid the unnecessary drama. Either way, self-control gives us space to make that decision.

It's important to note that self-control does not mean ignoring your feelings! It just means choosing to express our feelings in a way that reflects the kind of person we want to be in the world.

Let's face it: Sometimes, practicing self-control can be much harder to maintain in the heat of the moment. But the more you practice it, the better you get at staying calm under pressure and setting a good example for others.

Feeling angry or frustrated? Try counting to ten before reacting. Breathe through your nose and let yourself ground in the moment. Take this time to cool down and think before reacting, and instead respond in a way that is aligned with who you are trying to be. Don't let the anger control you; you control it.

3. Motivation: Sticking With It, Even When It's Hard

Motivation: what keeps you going, even when the going gets tough and overwhelming.

Motivation is an inner drive that pushes us to keep working toward something that matters. What's the key to staying motivated? Well, it's not just about forcing yourself to do things—it's about setting goals that *actually* excite you and breaking them down into manageable bite-sized pieces.

For instance, think about something you want to achieve: improving your grades, learning a new skill, or hitting a personal milestone. Motivation helps with focus and staying committed, even when the vibe just isn't there.

And, sometimes, just reminding yourself why you started can be the boost you need to keep going.

Try this: Write down one goal you want to reach and three small steps to get you started. Let's say you have always wanted to learn to play guitar—your three steps could be:

1. Find beginner lessons online
2. Practice for 15 minutes a day.
3. Learn one simple song by the end of the month.

As we can see, breaking your goal into smaller tasks makes it easier to stick with because you'll see the progress you're making along the way. Plus, checking things off your list feels great!

4. Empathy: Seeing the World Through Someone Else's Eyes

What is empathy? It is about understanding why a person you perceive as upset is feeling that way and showing them that you care. It's more than simply noticing someone struggling emotionally; it's like stepping into their shoes for a moment to see things from their perspective.

Let's break this down!

For example, your best friend is having a meltdown about an upcoming test. You have two courses of action that you could take. Instead of choice 1) casually brushing off their worries and telling them "They'll be fine," you could say for choice 2) "I can tell you're worried. Do you want to study together?" Small gestures like this can make a sizable difference in strengthening friendships and building trust.

Try this: The next time someone brings a problem to you that needs solving, really listen. Then, repeat what they've said in your words to ensure you understand. Active listening shows them you're paying attention and genuinely care about what they're going through.

Let's say a good friend tells you they're stressed out about an upcoming presentation. The same applies. Instead of responding with "You'll be fine," you could respond with, "So, you're feeling nervous about speaking in front of the class? We could practice together if you want."

This shows them that you're really listening and gives them a chance to open up more about what's bothering them.

When you take the time to acknowledge someone's feelings and offer encouragement, you're not just being kind—-you're strengthening your connection with them and demonstrating that you are a great communicator who cares about finding the solution to the problem.

5. Social Skills: Connecting With Others

Strong social skills help you communicate, build friendships, and work well as a member of a team. Whether you're leading a group project, resolving a disagreement, or just having a conversation, these skills make interactions smoother and, you guessed...more meaningful!

Knowing how to express yourself clearly, listen to others, and handle tricky social situations can make a big difference.

Try this: Practice making eye contact and offering a friendly smile next time you talk to someone. Whether you're meeting someone for the first time or simply chatting with a friend, making eye contact shows that you're engaged and interested in what they're saying.

But what if you're in a group? Try to make eye contact with each person as they speak—it helps build trust and makes for more natural-feeling conversations.

How to Build Your EQ

Step 1: Get to Know Your Emotions

It's not a secret that emotions don't just appear out of thin air —they're usually triggered by something happening around you, as we've seen. The better you understand what makes you feel happy, frustrated, excited, stressed, etc., the more control you'll have over the way you choose to react.

Let's think about it: What instantly puts you in a good mood?

Maybe it's hanging out with friends who always make you laugh, shopping, grabbing your favorite food and snacks, or finishing something you've worked really hard on.

Now, what tends to push your buttons?

- A rushed morning?
- A tough conversation?

Paying attention to these moments can help you predict how you'll react in different scenarios and give you the power to handle your emotions in a way that works for you.

Try this: For one week, write down one strong emotion you feel each day and what triggered it. Then, at the end of the week, see if you can spot the patterns.

Ask yourself, do certain things consistently make you feel stressed or energized?

- If you find that going for a short walk always boosts your mood, try making that a habit.
- If a particular type of conversation makes you anxious, consider how you could approach it differently next time.

Understanding yourself is the first step to managing your emotions and taking a leadership role in your own life.

Step 2: Stay Present with Mindfulness

Have you ever been so lost in your thoughts that you completely missed what someone just said? No worries— you're definitely not the only one!

But the even better news is that practicing mindfulness—being fully present in the moment—can help you stay much more focused, feel calmer, and handle stress much better.

Hear me out! Mindfulness doesn't mean you have to sit cross-legged and meditate for hours. Who even has time for that?

It can be as simple as taking a deep breath before that big test or paying close attention to the sounds and smells around you when you feel overwhelmed. The key here is that the more you practice grounding yourself in the present, the easier it becomes, even in stressful situations.

Try this: In a quiet spot, sit comfortably for two minutes.

Closing your eyes, try to focus on the rhythm of your breath-ing. Inhale slowly, and exhale gently through your mouth. If your mind wanders (which, let's be so for real, it will!), bring your focus back to your breath. Believe it or not, this tiny habit can help you feel closer and more in control throughout the day.

Step 3: Strengthen Your Relationships

Ever notice how some people seem to "get" others? They pick up on subtle clues—like a friend's slumped shoulders or a quiet, maybe distracted voice—and know precisely how to respond.

Have you ever wondered how they do that?

I'll let you in on a little secret—it's not magic—it's emotional intelligence (EQ) at work. And you can develop it, too!

For instance, the next time you talk to someone, pay close attention to their body language, tone of voice, and expressions. If a friend looks down or sounds tired, instead of assuming they're fine, you could ask, "Hey, you seem a little off today. Everything okay?" Small moments like this show people you care, which strengthens your relationships.

Try this: Do something kind for someone today—compliment a friend, help a classmate, or check in on someone and see how they're doing.

Notice how they respond. Do they smile? Relax a little?

The thing is, kindness is contagious! When you make someone feel good, you'll probably feel good, too.

Start Today!

The more you practice these habits, the easier they'll become. Remember, emotional intelligence isn't some mysterious trait; it's a set of skills built over time. And the best part? EQ will help you in every area of your life—friendships, school, work, and beyond!

Key Takeaways

- Emotional Intelligence helps you understand yourself and make solid connections with those in your life.
- Small habits like journaling, practicing mindfulness, and actively listening can greatly impact your relationships.

- EQ is a life skill that helps you make better decisions, be a strong leader, and stay calm under pressure.

The more you build on your EQ abilities, the easier life's challenges will feel. Keep exploring, keep learning, and see how these small changes will make a big impact!

2

CRITICAL THINKING

 "Education is not the learning of facts, but the training of the mind to think"

— ALBERT EINSTEIN

We've all been there—facing a tricky situation or trying to make a decision when you're not sure what to do. That, friends, is where critical thinking comes in! Think of it like having a built-in problem-solving toolkit. It helps you break things down, look at all angles, and make smart choices instead of just going with the first thing that pops into your head.

In this chapter, we'll explore critical thinking a bit more closely, why it's important, and how you can start using it in everyday life.

What Is Critical Thinking?

Critical thinking: the detective for your own thought! Instead of believing everything you see and hear at face value, critical thinking means you are stepping back, gathering information, and asking questions like: "Does this actually make sense?" or "Is there another way to look at this?"

It's all about thinking carefully before deciding what to believe and what action to take next.

Let's break this down for the ones in the back.

Let's say everyone is raving about a new restaurant in town, but when you check the reviews, some people have complained that it's overpriced and the service is not top-tier. Instead of blindly trusting the hype or dismissing the bad reviews altogether, you dig a little deeper and get more info.

You check the reviews, ask friends about their experiences, or even try it yourself to see what it's really like. That, in a nutshell, is critical thinking in action! You are weighing different perspectives and making an informed choice instead of jumping on the bandwagon or just guessing.

Figure 2.1 The essence of critical thinking lies in analyzing various factors before making informed decisions.

But critical thinking extends far beyond restaurant reviews. It's a fundamental skill that empowers you to navigate the complexities of daily life. Imagine encountering a news headline that screams a sensational claim.

A critical thinker wouldn't immediately share it. Instead, they'd consider the source, look for supporting evidence, and question potential biases. They'd ask: "Who benefits from this narrative?" or "Are there alternative explanations?"

You'd try to spot those sneaky arguments that try to fool you. For example, when someone says, "This celeb said it, so it must be true!" Even if they know nothing about the topic.

Plus, critical thinking means knowing you don't know everything.

It's like being cool with saying, "Maybe I'm wrong." It's about being open to other people's views and actually listening. It's realizing you might not have all the answers and being willing to change your mind if you find out something new.

Basically, it's about always learning and trying to figure out the real deal, even if it's hard.

It helps you not get tricked, solve problems better, and be a smarter person overall.

Why Does Critical Thinking Matter?

This skill is useful for way more than finding quality snacks or a great place to eat.

Imagine you're about to buy a video game. The trailer makes it look amazing, but the reviews say the game is full of glitches.

Do you throw caution to the wind and buy the game impulsively?

Nope! If you are critically thinking, you are doing your research, comparing experiences and opinions, and deciding if that information weighs in favor of the cost or not so much.

Critical thinking is also a skill that will back you up academically, within your friendships, and yes, even when planning out your future goals and dreams.

Let's say you're writing a history paper; critical thinking helps you weigh out which sources are most relevant to your topic versus wasting energy learning about information that will not help you in the short or long term.

If a friend tells you a shocking rumor—instead of blindly believing it, you ask, "Where did you hear that? Could there be more to the story?"

This way, you are avoiding misunderstandings, understanding that there are always more sides to a story than meets the eye, and by extension, you guessed it, this will help build stronger and more trusting relationships.

And building those trusting relationships? That's where critical thinking truly shines. It allows you to navigate the complex social landscape with greater awareness and sensitivity. It's not just about questioning information; it's about questioning assumptions, including your own.

Let's say, for example, if a disagreement arises with a friend, a critical thinker wouldn't immediately jump to conclusions or assign blame. They'd consider their own biases, acknowledge the friend's perspective, and seek common ground.

They'd ask things like, "What am I missing? What assumptions am I making?"

This self-awareness, coupled with a willingness to listen and understand, fosters an environment of mutual respect and open communication.

As a side quest, critical thinking equips you to recognize manipulative tactics and emotional manipulation. It's going to empower you to discern genuine intentions from hidden agendas.

In a world saturated with information and persuasive messages, the ability to analyze and evaluate claims is crucial for making informed decisions.

Essentially, critical thinking allows you to filter out the noise, identify reliable sources, and form your own independent judgments. This skill becomes paramount when considering life-altering choices, such as career paths, personal relationships, or financial investments.

For instance, what's the best way to invest your time and energy?

By cultivating critical thinking, you're not just improving your decision-making; you're building resilience, fostering self-reliance, and strengthening your ability to navigate the challenges and opportunities that life throws your way.

Between us, friends, this is a tool that empowers you to live more authentically and purposefully.

Common Myths About Critical Thinking

"You have to be a genius."

Nope! Not at all! Critical thinking isn't about being naturally gifted—it's a skill, much like we saw with mindfulness, that anyone can learn with practice. The more you use it, the easier it gets. Think of it like a muscle: the more you work it out, the stronger it becomes.

"Critical thinking just means finding mistakes."

Not at all! It's about tearing things apart—it's about being curious and open-minded. Instead of spotting problems, critical thinkers explore ideas and dig deeper to try to better understand something.

For example, let's imagine you're learning about personal finance.

Would it help to only think about the challenges of managing money?

Nope! You would want to ask questions such as, "What strategies can help build financial stability? How do different people successfully budget, save, and invest for their future?"

Thinking critically helps you see the full picture and make the most informed decision to serve your purpose well.

"It takes too long."

It might seem like extra work at fruits, but in the long run, critical thinking will actually save you time by helping you avoid bad decisions and the consequences that come with them.

Imagine you're writing a school paper and come across an article that seems, at face value, absolutely perfect!

Instead of rushing ahead, you take a minute to check: is this source reliable? If it turns out to be false information, you've just saved yourself an entire world of hurt by basing your argument on bad info—and from redoing the work later.

The moral of the story? A little extra leg work and upfront effort can save you a lot of headaches.

How To Think Smarter and Solve Problems Like A Pro

Not Everything You Read Is True—So How Do You Know What to Trust? The internet is full of wild headlines, bold claims, and flashy posts—but not all of it is accurate. So, how do you separate fact from fiction?

Let's paint a picture: You see a viral post that says, "Chocolate Cures Homework Stress!"

Sounds amazing, right? But, before you start stocking up on candy bars, you'll want to check if it's actually true, and you have to ask why. Where's the receipt? This is where you will analyze the information that's coming through.

- First, look at the source. Is it from a reliable website, a news organization, or a random social media account? A science journal saying dark chocolate may help with focus is very different from a meme claiming it's a magical stress cure.

- Second, check if other trustworthy sources say the same thing. If only one website makes the claim while others say the opposite, be skeptical. Reliable facts tend to show up in multiple places, not just one viral post.

- Next, watch out for emotional or exaggerated language. Words like "shocking," "mind-blowing," or "everything you know is a lie" are usually red flags. Good information is based on evidence, not hype.

- Finally, do a quick fact-check using different resources or even a simple Google search. If the claim holds up under scrutiny, great! If not, now you know better than to fall for the clickbait.

Being able to question and evaluate information is a super-power in today's world. The more you practice spotting reliable sources, the better you'll get at recognizing what's real and what's just noise.

How To Tell What's Real and What's Not

Spot the Bias

Have you ever read a review that's too good to be true? Maybe a new phone is being called the "greatest invention of all time," but the article forgets to mention a single downside. Well, a little digging might reveal that the writer works for the phone company. That friends...is bias!

So what do you do? Always ask: Who wants me to believe this? And why? What's the benefit of buying into this? What's being left out?

Thinking this way helps you see the bigger picture and avoid being misled.

Check the Source

Not all websites are created equal. A random blog post from "TottallyTruefcats.com" probably isn't as reliable as research from a university or a well-known (vetted) news source. But even trusted sources can make mistakes, so don't skim the headline—look at where they're getting their info. If an article isn't linked to any sources, that's a red flag!

Think of it like this: you wouldn't take medical advice from a random person on the street, right?

You'd want to hear from a doctor or a qualified professional. The same goes for information online. Just because it's on the internet doesn't mean it's true. You need to be a digital detective, sniffing out the real deal from the fake news.

And it's not just about obvious red flags like misspelled website names. Even seemingly legitimate sites can have biases or hidden agendas.

Yes, they might be trying to sell you something, promote a certain viewpoint, or even spread misinformation intentionally. That's why it's crucial to look beyond the surface and examine the source's credibility!

Ask yourself:

- Who created this website?
- What's their background?
- What are their credentials?
- Are they experts in the field they're writing about?

- Do they have a history of publishing accurate information?
- Most importantly, are they transparent about their sources?

A reliable source will always cite its information, providing links to original research, data, and other supporting materials.

This is so important because it allows you to verify the information for yourself and see if it holds up. If a website is vague or evasive about its sources, that's a major warning sign.

It's like a chef refusing to share their recipe —beware, something's definitely fishy!

Compare Different Perspectives

Two news sites report on the same event. One focuses on the economic impact, while the other highlights social consequences. By reading both (and checking more sources), you get a fuller picture of what's really happening.

If you only hear one side of the story, you could miss key details that form the bigger picture.

Solving Problems—Like a Boss

Life is full of challenges, big and small. No matter what stage of life you are at, critical thinking helps you break them down and handle them step-by-step—kind of like solving a puzzle!

Break It Down

Big problems can feel overwhelming, so take them one piece at a time. Say you and your friends are planning a school talent show. Instead of stressing over everything at once, list out the tasks you will need to complete in order to make the show run seamlessly.

- Pick a theme
- Find Performers
- Spread the word

Then, tackle each one in bite-sized pieces, and suddenly, it's not as intimidating after all!

Think of Different Solutions

The first idea isn't always the best one. If you need to save money, don't just decide, "I'll stop buying snacks." Think bigger! Can you shop during sales? Use coupons? Sell old stuff you don't use anymore for a few extra bucks? The more options you consider, the better your plan will be!

Learn from Mistakes

We've all tried something, failed miserably, and, yes, wanted to give up! Don't!

Mistakes are actually super useful—they show you what doesn't work so you can adjust. Let's say you're practicing for a school debate, and your argument falls flat. Instead of panicking, ask for feedback, find stronger evidence, and you got it, try again!

Think about athletes, musicians, or even your favorite content creators. Do you think they got everything right on the first try? Not a chance. Every missed goal, off-key note, or awkward first video was part of their learning process. The same applies to anything you're working on—school, friendships, jobs, or hobbies.

Instead of seeing mistakes as failures, treat them like checkpoints.

- What went wrong?
- What could be improved?

If you bomb a test, figure out what tripped you up and study differently next time. If a conversation doesn't go as planned, reflect on how you could communicate better.

The key is resilience. Every mistake means you're trying, learning, and getting closer to success. So, instead of beating yourself up, take a breath, adjust your approach, and keep moving forward!

Every mistake is a step toward getting better!

Making Smart Decisions

Good decisions don't just happen—you make them happen by thinking things through. Whether you're picking an extracurricular, deciding what to spend your money on, or figuring out weekend plans, these steps can help.

Make a List of Pros and Cons

Writing things down helps clear your head. Say you're trying to choose between the soccer team, the drama club, and the robotics team.

A quick list might look like this:

- Soccer Team: Great exercise, fun team atmosphere, scholarship opportunities, but huge time commitment.
- Drama Club: Boosts creative confidence and makes new friends but has long rehearsals on weekends.
- Robotics team: Cool STEM experience and build skills, but requires focus and late nights.

Now, you can clearly see what matters most and what works best for you!

Think About What's Most Important

Ask yourself: What do I actually enjoy? What fits my goals? If you love performing, drama club might be your thing. If you're into science and a die-hard for engineering, robotics could be a perfect fit. Choosing something that aligns with your interest makes it easier to stick with it and enjoy the experience.

Consider the Consequence!

Every choice has an impact. If you join the soccer team, will you have time for your homework and to study for tests? If you choose the drama club, will late rehearsals affect your sleep? Thinking ahead helps you avoid surprises and make a decision you won't regret.

Hands-On Learning: Think Smarter, Have Fun!

Want to sharpen your critical thinking skills? The best way to get better is to practice—but that doesn't mean it has to be boring! Here are some fun (and surprisingly useful) ways to boost your brainpower while enjoying yourself (actually).

Brain Games & Friendly Debates

Puzzles: Brain Workouts That Feel Like Play

Think of Sudoku, crosswords, or brain teasers as a gym for your mind. They help you spot patterns, think logically, and solve problems—all skills that come in handy in everyday life!

For example, solving Sudoku isn't just about filling in numbers; it's about planning ahead and figuring out what fits where without breaking the rules.

Crosswords? They stretch your vocabulary and force you to connect clues in creative ways. Plus, the more you practice, the quicker and sharper your thinking becomes.

Debates: The Art of Seeing Both Sides

Perhaps you've had a friendly argument over whether pineapple belongs on pizza? (Spoiler: it depends on who you ask!) Debating is an awesome way to see different perspectives, think fast, and make stronger arguments, reminding us that it's okay to agree to disagree!

Sometimes, it can only be pepperoni pie, and then you are aghast at the idea of a fruity Pizza, but for your best friend, it's something they can't live without.

To each their own!

Though pizza seems trivial, the point is this: Having the ability to craft a solid argument and view the issue from other perspectives is an invaluable tool that will carry you far in life!

Practice Activity

Pick a topic—like, "Should students have homework?" and argue both sides with a friend. For example, one side might say homework reinforces learning and teaches responsibility. Others might argue that it causes stress and takes away from personal time.

By looking at both arguments, you'll not only see things from a fresh angle but also get better at expressing your thoughts.

Who knows? You might even change your own mind!

Real-Life Thinking Challenges

Imagine you're throwing a class party; let's say it's the end-of-the-year graduation event of the year (literally). You need to decide on snacks, music, and activities.

Easy right?

Well, what if someone has food allergies? Or do all of your classmates have serious differences in what good music is? Now, you've got two problems to solve like a pro!

Instead of just guessing, you could survey your classmates to find out what snacks they like. If someone has a peanut allergy, you could make sure the food is safe for them. Then, think about setup—will you need decorations? Extra plates? By breaking it down step-by-step, you make sure everything runs smoothly and everyone has a great time.

Now, let's go even deeper.

What happens if the venue you plan to use is suddenly unavailable? A strong problem solver doesn't panic; they come up with alternatives. Maybe you can move the event outdoors or find a backup classroom. The key is thinking ahead and preparing for challenges before they turn into full-blown disasters.

And let's not forget teamwork! You don't have to do everything alone. Delegating tasks—like asking one friend to handle music and another to organize games—makes the whole process smoother. Plus, working together builds collaboration skills that will come in handy for future projects, jobs, and, well... life in general.

Planning a party may seem like just a fun event, but it's actually a great exercise in decision-making, organization, and problem-solving. The more you practice tackling challenges like these, the easier it will be to handle bigger, real-world situations in the future.

The Rumor Mill as a Critical Thinker

Ben is quitting the soccer team- the rumor has it that he got in a huge fight with the coach. Instead of believing it (or spreading it), stop and think:

- Where did this come from?
- Is it firsthand knowledge, or just gossip?
- Can I check with a reliable source—like speaking directly to Ben?

If it turns out to be false, you just prevented unnecessary drama. And if it's true, now you know the facts without jumping to conclusions. Thinking before racing is a game changer in avoiding unnecessary stress!

Creative Thinking Games

"What if?" –The Game of Endless Possibilities

What if you had to build a treehouse but could only use three tools? Which ones would you pick? A hammer, a saw, and nails? Okay, now what if you could only have two tools?

How would you adapt?

Playing the "what if?" games forces you to think outside the box and find creative solutions. It's a fun way to develop problem-solving skills—whether you're brainstorming an invention, planning a trip, or figuring out how to fix something without all the right tools.

Mind Mapping: The Ultimate Idea Organizer

What do you do when there are a bunch of ideas swirling around in your head, but you don't know where to start? Try mind mapping!

1. Write your main idea in the center of the page (Ex. Science fair project)
2. Draw branches with related topics, such as space exploration, human biology, or physics experiments.
3. Keep adding smaller branches for more specific ideas. Like adding "Rocket Propulsion" or "Gravity Simulation" under the heading Space Exploration)

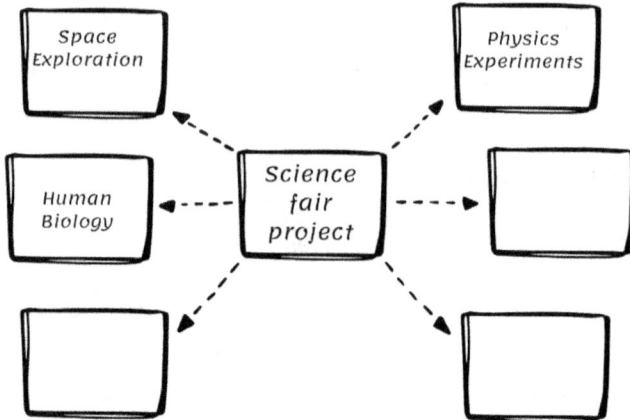

Figure 2.1 *A visual representation of mind mapping, where a central idea branches out into related topics and subtopics.*

Reverse Thinking: Solve Problems Backward

Instead of asking, "How do I make this project successful?" flip it: "What could go wrong and ruin it?'

Say you're working on a group project. What's the worst that could happen?

- People don't communicate.
- Roles aren't clear.
- Someone forgets their part on presentation day.

Now that you know the potential issues, you can prevent them by setting clear roles and keeping communication open. Reverse thinking is a lot like finding weak spots in a plan before they become real problems!

Critical thinking isn't about memorizing facts—it's about learning how to think smarter in any situation. Whether you're solving puzzles, planning a party, or deciding if a rumor is true, these strategies will help you make better choices and avoid mistakes.

Key Takeaways

- Practice with Puzzles, debates, and creative thinking games
- Break down big problems into smaller steps
- Question information before receiving it.
- Stay open-minded—there's always more than one presumptive!

So, next time you're faced with a tricky decision, a mystery to solve, or a problem to untangle, put those critical thinking skills to work—and have fun while you're at it!

3

COMMUNICATION SKILLS

 "The most important thing in communication is hearing what isn't said."

— PETER DRUCKER

Honestly—communication is everything! Being able to communicate well is one of the most valuable skills you will ever have. It's how you make friends, share ideas, and solve problems.

If you can express yourself clearly, you'll be able to connect with others and navigate situations with ease. Without solid communication, things can get complicated really fast, and misunderstandings happen more often.

Think about how much easier life would be if you could confidently explain your thoughts in class, have smooth conversations with your friends and family, or even give a presentation without feeling nervous or unprepared. When you know how to communicate well, those situations become a lot less intimidating. The more you practice, the better you'll get at expressing yourself and the more confident you'll feel.

Communication is all around us—when you chat face-to-face, send a text, or post on social media. Each form has its own style, but the goal is always the same: to be clear and understood. When you're good at it, everything from building relationships to excelling at work becomes a lot easier.

In this chapter, we'll dive into why communication is so important, how to improve the way we share our messages, and, most importantly, some fun ways to practice! You'll get tips and exercises that'll make learning to communicate better feel like an exciting challenge.

Why Communication Is Key

Good communication is the key to working well with others, leading a group, and building strong relationships. If you can explain your thoughts clearly—whether you're planning a group project or just hyping up a friend— you create trust and understanding. But communication isn't just about talking; it's also about listening, responding, and making sure everyone feels heard.

When you're a strong communicator, you can better handle disagreements, get your ideas across, and make your everyday interactions more meaningful.

By actively listening, you show that you value others' perspectives, which encourages open dialogue and mutual respect.

In any situation, whether at work or with friends, a strong communicator can make a big difference. You can handle disagreements more effectively by staying calm, keeping an open mind, and focusing on finding a solution instead of escalating the issue.

When you listen thoughtfully and express yourself clearly, it's easier to make your ideas stick and gain support from others. Plus, strong communication helps in navigating difficult conversations or resolving conflicts without causing unnecessary stress or frustration.

The ability to communicate well also creates more meaningful interactions in your everyday life. Whether you're giving feedback, asking for help, or just catching up with a friend, being able to convey your thoughts clearly and respectfully strengthens relationships.

Good communication builds the foundation for trust, allowing others to feel comfortable sharing their thoughts with you, leading to deeper and more genuine connections.

Communication in Leadership and Teamwork

Great leaders all have one thing in common: they know how to communicate. They can break things down in a way that makes sense, inspire people, and *actually* listen to what others have to say.

Think about a time someone explained something so well that everything just clicked—it made your life easier, right? Now, imagine the opposite: being in a group where no one knows what is going on because instructions aren't clear.

That's what happens when communication goes south.

When you're working on a group project, for example, or you are at work, collectively trying to find a solution to a problem, clear communication helps the team stay organized, while poor communication leads to frustration and missed deadlines.

The Three Types of Communication

Verbal Communication

This is anything spoken—whether it's having a conversation, telling a story, or giving a speech. The way you say something can completely change how people understand it.

Imagine telling someone about an amazing vacation you've just come home from.

If you only say, "It was cool," chances are they probably won't be super stocked to hear the rest of your story. But, if you said, "We sat around the campfire, roasting marshmallows under the stars," you're painting a picture that draws them in.

The words you choose and how you say them—like your tone, excitement, or emphasis–make a huge difference.

Non-Verbal Communication

This is everything you communicate without speaking—your body language, facial expressions, gestures, and even posture. You can say you're fine, but if your arms are crossed and you won't make eye contact...it's saying, "I don't care."

Sometimes, a simple nod shows you're listening, while smiling makes you seem friendly and approachable. On the other hand, slouching might make you look bored, and avoiding eye contact can make you seem unsure of yourself—Confidence is key!

Being aware of these subtle cues can help make sure your words and actions measure up!

Written Communication

Writing isn't just for essays and schoolwork—it's everywhere! Emails, texts, social media posts, and even quick notes all require the ability to communicate clearly. In fact, how you write plays a huge role in avoiding misunderstandings, and it's something we all use in our daily lives. For example, if you simply text, "See ya later," it can leave the other person wondering, "When? Where?" But if you add more specifics, like "Meet me at the library at 4 pm," there's no room for confusion. The clearer you are, the better your communication will be!

When it comes to emails, which we'll discuss in more detail, starting with a polite greeting—like "Hi [Name]" or "Dear [Name]"—is a good way to set the right tone. Then, make sure you clearly state your point early on.

For example, if you're writing to ask about a meeting, you might start with, "I'm writing to inquire about the meeting scheduled for next week." This tells the reader right away what the email is about. Clear, concise writing helps the person on the other end understand exactly what you're asking or sharing and ensures you get the response you're looking for.

If you're using social media, being clear also matters. While you can be casual, it's still important to be thoughtful and avoid leaving things open to misinterpretation. A simple message like "Can't wait to catch up with everyone at 6 pm tonight!" helps everyone stay on the same page. Communication is key, and a little extra clarity can go a long way in keeping things smooth and stress-free!

Becoming a Better Communicator

Great communication skills take time and practice, but improving a little day by day makes a huge difference. Whether it's speaking up in class, texting more clearly, or practicing how you tell stories, every effort helps. Here's how you can level up in different areas:

Verbal Communication

Public Speaking Tips

Talking in front of others can be nerve-wracking, but the more you practice, the less overwhelming it will feel. Start by practicing in front of a mirror or perhaps a family member or friend. You might feel awkward at first, but remember, everyone starts somewhere! The more comfortable you become, the easier it will be to speak confidently in front of larger audiences.

When you're ready to step it up, use simple and clear words that will ensure your message is understood. You don't need to complicate things—getting to the point is often the best approach. If you get nervous, take slow, deep breaths. This can help calm your nerves and prevent your thoughts from racing. You can also imagine the scenario as if you're just having a conversation with a friend—informal, relaxed, and not a big deal. This shift in perspective can help reduce the pressure and make the experience feel more natural.

Remember, confidence comes with practice. Start small—maybe by answering questions in class or speaking up during a group discussion. It's a great way to get comfortable with expressing yourself in front of others. Don't be afraid to make mistakes! Each step you take is a win, and every time you speak up, you're building confidence. Your voice matters, and you deserve to be heard! So, take a deep breath, trust yourself, and keep practicing!

Storytelling

A good story, as we saw above, will start out with a hook, yes, but it's not just about 'what happened.' Storytelling, at its core, is about inspiring people to feel something. By adding details and emotions, your stories will come to life, and your audience will, too!

Let's break it down with a quick example!

Instead of saying simply, "We went to the park," try saying something that will pull the audience into the scene with you. For example, "The sunset had turned the sky to pink and orange; there was a cool breeze that rustled past the leaves. My little brother tore past me, screaming until it happened..."

Naturally, your audience will want to know...What happened?"

That is the art of storytelling; never give away your whole hand at once! Pace yourself and actively engage with those around you. Engaging details make your audience feel like they were there with you; in this case, they heard your brother screaming as he ran past, heard the wind rustling in the trees, and saw with their own eyes the way the sun was setting.

It's all in the details!

Persuasion Skills

Do you want to make a convincing case for something? Let's say you're trying to convince your parents to give you an extended curfew. The trick isn't in being stubborn or demanding—it's about understanding their point of view first! Instead of immediately cutting them off or getting defensive, you have the chance to really change their mind by approaching the situation from a different angle.

Let's take a typical example:

"I'd like to stay out until eight o'clock on the weekend."

"No, that's way too late!"

Now, if you were to immediately respond with "You're wrong!" or "That's not fair!" you've just hit a dead end. That's the last thing you want when trying to persuade someone. The conversation is over, and you've pushed your chance of persuasion way down the drain.

But let's try this instead:

"I work until 6 pm on Saturdays. I'd like to be able to see my friends before coming home. Is it reasonable that I could have an extra hour? I have to be at soccer practice at 9 am Sunday and back at work at 2 pm, so this is really my only free time."

This time, you're offering a well-thought-out reason for why you're asking. You're showing that you understand their concern—late nights can be a problem—while also offering a solution that's grounded in facts and context. You're not just asking for something out of the blue; you're showing that you've thought it through. You're offering a clear and calm explanation, and you've set the tone for a conversation, not a confrontation.

This type of approach can be used in many different situations, from negotiating at work to persuading friends to try a new idea. The key is to avoid becoming defensive or combative. Instead, offer reasons and ideas that invite thoughtfulness and reflection. By presenting your perspective in a way that's respectful and backed by logical reasoning, you can often inspire change more effectively than through frustration or forcefulness.

Remember, it's not about forcing your point of view; it's about guiding the other person to see your side and doing so in a way that leaves room for understanding and compromise. People are more likely to be persuaded when they feel heard and when the conversation feels like a two-way street.

Non-Verbal Communication

Body language

As we briefly discussed above, how you carry yourself says a lot before you even open your mouth. Standing tall shows confidence, while slouching might make you seem uninterested or even sad!

While using natural hand gestures can help you emphasize a point when you're speaking, avoid fidgeting or crossing your arms because you are likely showing the people around you that you are nervous or closed off.

In a group setting, leaning in slightly shows you're engaged, while sitting too far back can make you seem disconnected.

Paying attention to your body language greatly impacts how people perceive you.

Eye Contact

Remember, looking a person in the eye while talking to them shows you are paying attention and makes you seem more confident. If you're speaking to a group, try to make eye contact with different people so everyone feels included.

If you're nervous, a good trick is to look at someone's forehead or between their eyebrows—it still gives the impression of eye contact without feeling too intense.

Facial expressions

Your face should match the mood of what you're saying. If you're excited about an instance, you're probably smiling, and your eyebrows will be raised. If you're discussing something serious, keep your expression calm, neutral, and, most of all, focused on the message; if there seems to be a mismatch between your words and your expression—like smiling while giving bad news—- it can be confusing or even come across as insincere.

Written Communication

Writing Clear Emails

A good email goes a long way! It gets to the point quickly without being too wordy or confusing.

A great email starts with a clear subject line like, "Science Club meeting this Friday."

Be polite and direct in your body — "Hey everyone, just confirming the meeting at the library at 3 pm for the science club weekly meeting."

If you're asking for something, make sure it's clear. A good practice is to ask questions. Who? Where? What? When? How?

Ending an email with "Doors open at 6 pm. RSVP as soon as possible." helps keep things friendly and open-ended.

Texting and messages

Even casual messages should be clear enough to avoid misunderstandings. Instead of saying, "See you later," try just like emails, being specific; "Meet me at 3 pm outside the gym; we'll get coffee after that."

Being specific helps avoid confusion. In group texts, listing details—like what to bring, where to go, and arrival time—keeps everyone on the same page.

Fun Ways to Practice Communication

Getting better at communication doesn't have to leave you baffled or be boring! Try these activities:

- Role-Playing Conflict Resolution: Act out different situations with friends to practice handling disagreements calmly.
- Public Speaking games: Take turns giving short speeches about random topics you find interesting.
- Storytelling Challenges: Try telling a story using only five sentences—see who can make theirs the most interesting!

- Social Media Etiquette: Talk about how messages can be misinterpreted online and brainstorm ways to communicate more clearly.

Key Takeaways

- Communication is essential for building relationships, finding solutions, and working in teams.
- Verbal, nonverbal, and written communication all play a big role in how we connect with others.
- Practicing real-life situations makes communication skills fun and effective.

By improving your communication skills, you'll not only express yourself more clearly but also strengthen your relationships and make everyday interactions smoother and more enjoyable!

4

THE TECH MASTER

"Once a new technology rolls over you, if you're not part of the steamroller, you're part of the road."

— STEWART BRAND

Technology is everywhere! Whether you're binge-watching your fav series, texting memes, or cramming for an exam, tech does make our lives so much easier! But you know what? Using it isn't enough—you need to know how to use it well.

Having the right tech skills is no joke. It can help you work smarter, not harder, help keep yourself safe, and open doors to future opportunities.

There's so much to unpack in this chapter, so let's look at key tech skills that set you up for success!

Think about it: simply knowing how to scroll through TikTok isn't the same as understanding how algorithms shape your feed. Being tech-savvy means grasping the underlying mechanics, from basic troubleshooting to navigating complex software. It's about recognizing online threats, like phishing scams or data breaches, and knowing how to protect your personal information.

Also, it's important to realize that tech skills aren't just about using existing tools; they're about adapting to the ever-changing digital landscape. For instance, coding, data analysis, and even digital content creation are becoming increasingly valuable in various fields. Learning these skills can not only enhance your current studies but also prepare you for future careers that might not even exist yet.

So what's tech really about? It's about embracing digital literacy as a fundamental life skill, one that empowers you to thrive in a technology-driven world.

Staying Safe & Protecting Your Identity

The internet is awesome! You can connect with friends and learn new things. Can we shout out the cute cat videos? But just like in real life, there are risks—so protecting your personal info is a MUST!

Think of online security as locking your front door; you wouldn't leave it wide open for anyone to walk in, right?

Here's how to keep your digital life safe and sound:

1. Use a strong password

A weak password is like using a sticky note as a door lock—it won't stop anyone and could result in sensitive and important information falling into the wrong hands. Trust me, you would not want to wake up to a drained bank account! Here's how to create one that works:

- Mix uppercase + lowercase letters, numbers, and symbols.
- Don't use anything obvious (like your name, birthday, or "password123").
- Use a different password for every account (a password manager can help you keep track).
- Weak Passwords: 123456, password, qwerty
- Strong passwords: Tr33House_9&7, P@ssw0rd!2024

2. Watch out for Scams

Ever get a sketchy email saying your bank account is locked or that you have won a million dollars? That's phishing—when scammers try to trick you into giving up personal info.

Red Flags to watch for:

- Strange email addresses that don't match the company's real domain.
- Generic greetings like "Dear Customer" instead of an actual name.
- Urgent messages pressuring you to click a link now!

Pro tip: If you get a weird message, don't click anything. Instead, go directly to the company's official site to check if it's legitimate.

3. Check Your Privacy Settings

Most apps and social media platforms let you control who sees your info—so use those settings!

Why it matters:

- Public profiles leave you open to strangers (hello, random DMs).
- Location tracking can reveal more than you want.
- Future employers or schools might see posts you didn't mean to share.

Take five minutes today to review your privacy settings—you'll thank yourself later.

4. Be Smart About Public Wi-fi

Free Wi-fi at coffee shops or airports? Fantastic— love that for you! Hackers...they also love that for you and wouldn't mind lifting your data.

Stay safe with these tips:

- Avoid logging into your bank accounts or sensitive sites while using public wi-fi.
- Use a VPN to encrypt your connection.
- If you must use public wi-fi, stick to trusted networks (and don't auto-connect!).

Mastering Virtual Meetings & Team Communication

Whether it's for school, work, or a group project, knowing how to communicate well on one is a game changer.

Keeping Teams in Check

Platforms like Slack, Teams, and Discord are awesome for collabs—but only if used the right way.

- Keep messages short and clear—get to the point!
- Use threads or separate channels for different topics.
- Tag people only when necessary (nobody likes notification overload).
- Bad messages: "Hey...um, so I was thinking maybe we should start the project soon?"
- Better message: "Hey @team, let's set a deadline for the first draft—how about Friday?"

Virtual Meeting Do's & Don'ts

Want to nail your next Zoom call? Follow these easy rules;

- Mute when you're not speaking. No one wants to hear the dog barking!
- Check your background. If your space is giving "Clean up on aisle 5," try using a virtual one.
- Stay engaged. No scrolling social media sites; give respect, get respect.

Bonus tip: If you're leading a call, come prepared! Have an agenda so the meeting stays on track!

Practice Activity

- Update your passwords–make sure they're strong and unique.

- Enable two-factor authentication (2FA) for extra security.
- Take an online phishing quiz to test your ability to spot the scams.
- Check the privacy settings on three of your favorite apps.
- Host a virtual meeting with friends to practice online communication skills.

By building these skills, you'll navigate technology like a pro—staying safe, working smarter, not harder, and making the most of every tool at your fingertips.

Making Sense of Data: The Basics

Have you ever noticed how your favorite apps always seem to recommend the perfect song or suggest products you were just talking about? That's the magic of data in action!

Understanding how to interpret data can help you spot patterns, make better choices, and even solve everyday problems more effectively.

Types of Data

Data comes in two primary forms: quantitative and qualitative. Let me explain!

- **Quantitative data** is all about numbers and measurements—like how many steps you take each day or how many hours you spend on any social media app.

- **Qualitative data** focuses on descriptions and characteristics, such as your favorite apps and why you enjoy using them.

For example, tracking how much time you spend reading this book would be quantitative, while explaining what you like about the book would be qualitative,

So what's the point? Both data sets help us analyze trends, make informed decisions, and find solutions to different aspects of life.

Spotting Patterns in Data

One thing about data is that it can reveal trends in your daily habits. You might even notice that you spend more time on social media at night or that your gaming hours spike on Tuesdays. Recognizing these patterns can help you make wise choices—like setting screen time limits or planning breaks between study sessions. By analyzing your data, you gain insights that can definitely improve your time management—it's a win!

Seeing The Vision

So, what's the best way to turn visuals like data into something we can digest? Since we eat with our eyes...turning numbers into visuals like charts and graphs makes those patterns nice and straightforward to understand.

Side quest: Make them colorful! Feel free to be as creative as your heart desires!

Google Sheets and Excel can help you create graphs and tables that display your data clearly.

Here's how:

- Enter your data into a spreadsheet (e.g., hours spent on different activities each day.)
- Highlight your data and use the chart tools (in the home banner) to create a graph.
- Choose a format that best displays your information —pie charts for app usage, bar graphs for weekly trends, etc.
- Customize colors, labels, and titles to make them visually appealing and easily read.

	School	Homework	Sports/Exercise	Social Media	Gaming	Sleep	Other
Monday	6	2	1	3	2	8	2
Tuesday	6	2	1	3	2	8	2
Wednesday	6	2	1	3	2	8	2
Thursday	6	2	1	3	2	8	2
Friday	6	2	1	3	2	8	2
Saturday	0	1	2	4	3	9	5
Sunday	0	1	2	4	3	9	5

Figure 4.1 *A daily tracker spreadsheet displaying time allocation for various activities.*

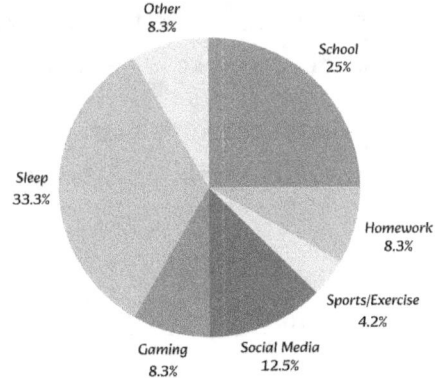

Figure 4.2 *A pie chart illustrating the distribution of activities for a weekday.*

How does this help?

A pie chart showing how you divide your time between home-work, social media, and gaming can give you a clear picture of your daily habits. These tools simplify it, turning data into something you can bite on!

Practice Activity

- Track how you spend your time each week.
- Create a chart showing how much time is distributed across the different activities in your life.
- Reflect on your data usage. See if you can make one or two adjustments that make sense for your lifestyle and make for a more balanced mindset.

The Rise of AI

Artificial intelligence (AI) isn't a futuristic concept—it's already part of your daily life.

Whether it's a streaming platform for shows or movies, your phone autocorrecting or predicting text, or grammar software suggesting their best version of the text you've written, AI is working behind the scenes to make life easier.

But, just like our internet discussion, learning to use AI in a way that aligns with your daily goals and tasks will be a huge benefit!

Key Types of AI and How They Work

Generative: This type of AI essentially creates new content based on patterns that it has learned. Tools like ChatGPT can, for instance, help with writing, generating ideas, or even asking for lecture summaries on complex concepts. The list is too big for our purpose here, but hop on and check it out; you will not be sorry!

Predictive: This AI's job is to analyze past data and use that information to make predictions. For instance, businesses use it to understand customer preferences, and meteorologists use it for weather forecasts.

Computer Vision: This AI specializes in interpreting visual info. Essentially, it helps things like self-driving cars recognize objects, assists in things like medical imaging, and powers tools like Face ID, which we all use daily.

Natural Language Processing (NLP): This AI allows machines to understand and process human language. What does that mean? Think about the voice commands you give your phones or writing tools for grammar and spelling checks on your schoolwork documents.

Practice Activity

- Find one thing in your life that AI could help with (homework, scheduling, content creation, etc.)
- Try out an AI tool to save time or boost productivity.
- Reflect on how it worked and what else you could use it for.

Keeping UP With Technology

It's no joke—tech is constantly changing! The best way to stay ahead of the game is to keep learning and evolving alongside it!

- Follow Tech Blogs & Podcasts: Check out sources like TechCrunch and Wired, or follow tech Youtubers to stay in the loop.
- Take an online course: Platforms like Coursera and Khan Academy offer various free coding, AI, and design resources.
- Join online Communities: Engaging in tech forums, Discord groups, or Reddit threads helps you learn from others and share insights.

Key Takeaways

- Spotting patterns in your data helps you make a smarter decision
- AI tools can save time and boost productivity when used the right way.
- Keeping up with technology ensures you are ready and stay ready for the future!

Master these skills, and you'll be set to navigate the digital world like a master!

ADAPTABILITY AND RESILIENCE

 "Life doesn't get easier or more forgiving, we get stronger and more resilient."

— STEVE MARABOLI

Alright, buckle up, buttercups, because life's about to get real!

Life has a funny way of throwing surprises at us— sometimes, when we least expect it! Whether it's a pop quiz at school, an unexpected shift change at work, or maybe it's just one of those days when everything seems to go wrong, being able to roll with the punches can make a huge difference!

Seriously though, think of adaptability as having a mental "undo" button for those moments when things go sideways. You know, when your phone decides to die right before you need directions or when your perfectly planned hangout gets rained out? It's about being able to switch gears, find a Plan B (or even a Plan C!), and not letting a little bump in the road derail your whole vibe.

And resilience? That's your superhero cape! It's bouncing back from those tough moments, dusting yourself off, and saying, "Alright, life, you tried it, but I'm not giving up!" It's like when you mess up a recipe, but instead of throwing the whole thing in the trash, you experiment and create something even better. Talk about a comeback!

But the real secret sauce? That's the positive mindset!

It's about seeing the silver lining, even when it's hiding behind a big, gloomy cloud. It's about laughing at your own mistakes, finding the humor in the chaos, and remembering that even the worst days have something good in them.

Imagine you spill coffee on your favorite shirt. Instead of freaking out, you decide it now has a "unique, abstract design," and suddenly you're a fashion icon. See? Positivity for the win! Ultimately, we want to see you thriving, no matter what life throws your way, so let's get ready to make those lemons into some seriously delicious lemonade!

In Chapter Five, we are doing a deep dive into leveling up your adaptability game, resilience, and positive mindset because... we love that for you!

Adaptability and Resilience: What's Up With That?

I'm glad you asked! Adaptability is all about going with the flow and, as the name suggests, adjusting to changes that come your way with a positive attitude.

It's what helps us figure out new apps on our phones or find our way to a restaurant when, say, our maps aren't working right.

Resilience means different things for everyone, and we all do it differently. But it can be as simple as getting used to a new school or job as much as finding creative ways to tackle unexpected bumps in the road.

Basically, it's your superpower, equipping you to handle change smoothly and with confidence.

When you combine adaptivity and resilience, you become unstoppable—able to handle challenges, grow from them— and not feel defeated and give up.

Think of adaptability like being a chameleon, you know? You just blend into whatever situation you're in. Maybe your favorite hangout spot closes down? No sweat! You're already brainstorming new places to chill with your friends. Or maybe your usual study routine gets thrown off by a surprise project? You're like, "Alright, let's switch it up!" and find a new way to get things done. It's about being flexible and not getting stuck in your ways.

And resilience? That's like your personal bounce-back meter. Do you know those times when you totally bombed a test or got cut from the team? Instead of just wallowing in disappointment, you're like, "Okay, that sucked, but what can I learn from this?" You pick yourself up, figure out what went wrong, and come back stronger. It's about not letting setbacks define you. It's about turning those "oops" moments into "aha!" moments.

And here's the cool part: when you mix these two superpowers, you become a total force of nature. You can handle anything life throws your way, from awkward social situations to major life changes. You're not just surviving; you're thriving. You're learning, growing, and becoming a better version of yourself. And honestly, who wouldn't want that? It's like having a cheat code for life, but way more fun and way more rewarding.

Why These Skills Matter

First off, life isn't a straight line. It's more like a rollercoaster designed by a mischievous squirrel – full of unexpected twists, turns, and the occasional terrifying drop! Adaptability is your seatbelt on that ride.

It's what keeps you from flying off the rails when things don't go according to plan. Think about it: plans change, people change, and sometimes, your favorite burrito joint closes down (tragedy!). Without adaptability, you'd be stuck, frustrated, and maybe even a little hangry. But with it, you're like, "Alright, new burrito place, here I come!" You can navigate the unexpected, find solutions, and keep moving forward.

Now, let's talk about resilience. This is your personal armor against the inevitable bumps and bruises of life. You know those moments when you feel like you've hit rock bottom? Maybe you failed a test, got rejected from your dream job, or had a friendship fall apart. Resilience is what helps you pick yourself up, dust yourself off, and keep going.

This is definitely not about pretending everything's fine; it's about acknowledging the pain, learning from the experience, and coming back stronger. Imagine a rubber band – it stretches and bends, but it always snaps back. That's resilience. It allows you to bounce back from setbacks, learn from your mistakes, and build mental toughness.

Why are these skills so crucial?

Well, for starters, they boost your mental and emotional well-being! When you're adaptable, you're less stressed and anxious because you're confident in your ability to handle whatever comes your way. And when you're resilient, you're less likely to get bogged down by negativity and self-doubt.

You develop a sense of inner strength and confidence that allows you to face challenges with a positive attitude.

Believe me when I say these skills are essential for success in all areas of life. You can be navigating school, work, or relationships, and adaptability and resilience will give you a significant advantage.

In today's fast-paced, ever-changing world, employers are looking for people who can think on their feet, solve problems creatively, and adapt to new situations. In your personal life, these skills will help you build stronger relationships, overcome obstacles, and achieve your goals.

Adaptability and resilience foster personal growth, pushing you outside your comfort zone, encouraging you to try new things, and helping you to discover your hidden potential. When you're willing to embrace change and face challenges head-on, you're constantly learning and evolving. You become more self-aware, more resourceful, and more confident in your abilities.

Finally, these skills are always going to contribute to a happier, more fulfilling life, no matter which way you want to slice that pie up!

When you're adaptable and resilient, you're less likely to get stuck in a rut or feel overwhelmed by life's challenges. You're able to embrace change, find joy in the present moment, and create a life that's truly meaningful to you. Ultimately, adaptability and resilience aren't just skills; they're superpowers that empower you to live your best life.

So, why should you care about adaptability and resilience? Because they help you not just survive challenges but thrive in the face of them.

Here's how:

Cool Under Pressure

Life is unpredictable, and sometimes things won't go as planned. Adaptability helps you stay calm and think on your feet. Imagine you're all set to present a group project, but a key teammate is out sick.

Instead of panicking, you adapt—maybe you cover their part or tweak the presentation on the fly. Being flexible under pressure helps keep stress levels low and confidence high.

Reaching Your Goals

Resilience keeps you moving forward, even when things get tough. Learning a new skill, improving in a subject, or training for a sport takes effort.

It's easy to feel frustrated when progress is slow, but resilience keeps you going.

For example, if math isn't your strong suit, resilience pushes you to keep practicing, ask for help, and try new strategies until you get it. Every setback is just another step toward success!

It's not about having a perfect life; it's about growing where you're planted, even when the conditions aren't ideal. We've all been there, right? You're trying to learn a new video game, and you keep getting owned by the same boss. Or you're trying to nail that perfect guitar riff, and your fingers just won't cooperate.

That's when resilience kicks in.

It's like having a mental "retry," but instead of just restarting the level, you're learning from your mistakes. It's about saying, "Okay, that didn't work, let's try something else." Maybe you watch a tutorial, ask a friend for tips, or just take a break and come back with a fresh perspective. It's not about being perfect; it's about being persistent.

And let's be honest, sometimes the best part of reaching a goal is the journey, not just the destination. It's about the small victories, the little "aha" moments, and the feeling of accomplishment when you finally figure something out. It's about proving to yourself that you're capable of more than you thought. So, next time you're feeling frustrated, remember that little sapling pushing through the concrete. Keep pushing, keep trying, and keep growing. You got this!

Boosting Confidence

Every time you overcome a challenge, you prove to yourself that you can handle tough situations. If you power through a difficult situation, you gain even more self-confidence. The more challenges you tackle, the stronger and more self-assured you become.

We could think of it like leveling up in a video game, but instead of digital points, you're getting real-life experience and a serious dose of "I got this!" vibes. Seriously, think about it. That time you aced a presentation you were dreading? Or, finally, learn that tricky skateboard trick? Those moments aren't just about the achievement; they're like little confidence injections.

And here's the cool thing: the more you do it, the easier it gets. You start to realize that even when things seem impossible, you've got the tools and the grit to figure it out. It's like building a mental muscle; the more you use it, the stronger it gets. It's not about being fearless; it's about knowing that even when you're scared, you can handle it.

The Power of Positive Thinking

Staying positive doesn't mean pretending everything is sunshine and rainbows. It just means focusing on what you can control and looking for the good in every situation.

Instead of thinking, "I can't do this," try, "I'll give it my best shot and see what happens."

That slight shift in mindset makes a huge difference. A positive outlook helps you stay motivated, think more clearly, and find creative solutions when problems arise. Over time, this makes bouncing back from setbacks so much easier.

See, it's not about ignoring the bad stuff. It's about not letting it completely take over your brain. It's like spilling coffee on your favorite shirt before a big presentation. Yeah, that sucks.

But instead of spiraling into a "my whole day is ruined" melt-down, you're like, "Okay, stain stick, where are you?" Or, you know, "This shirt now has character!" It's about choosing your reaction.

And honestly, our brains are kinda like toddlers – they believe what you tell them. If you keep saying, "I'm gonna fail," your brain's gonna be like, "Alright, sounds good!" But if you switch it up and say, "I'm gonna try my best, and even if I mess up, I'll learn something," your brain's like, "Cool, let's do this!" It's about giving yourself permission to try, even if you're not 100% sure you'll succeed.

Plus, when you're in a positive headspace, you're way more creative. You're not so focused on the problem that you can't see the solutions. It's like when you're trying to solve a puzzle. If you're stressed out, you're just gonna stare at the pieces and get nowhere. But if you take a deep breath and relax, you might see a pattern you missed before.

And here's the best part: it's a skill you can build. Like, you don't just wake up one day and become a positivity ninja. It takes practice. Start small. Instead of complaining about some-thing, try to find one thing you're grateful for. Or, when you catch yourself thinking negatively, try to reframe it into some-thing more positive.

It's also about surrounding yourself with positive people. You know, the ones who lift you up and make you feel good about yourself. Avoid the energy vampires who are always complaining and bringing you down. Find your tribe, the people who believe in you and support your dreams.

Ultimately, positive thinking isn't about ignoring reality; it's about choosing how you react to it. It's about recognizing that you have the power to control your thoughts and emotions, even when things get tough. And that, my friends, is a super-power worth having.

Embracing a Growth Mindset

A growth mindset means believing you will get better at anything with effort and practice. Instead of saying, "I'm just bad at math," you say, "I'm working on improving my math skills." That small change in thinking keeps you from giving up when things get tough.

If you struggle with a sports drill, a new language, or a creative project, a growth mindset encourages you to keep trying, seek feedback, and celebrate progress.

Every challenge becomes a stepping stone instead of a road-block. The best part? The more you practice this mindset, the easier it gets to push through tough moments.

Setting Goals That Work

Big dreams are awesome but can feel overwhelming if you try to tackle everything at once. The secret? Break them down into smaller, manageable steps.

Let's say you want to boost your grades. Instead of stressing over the entire semester, start with simple goals—like studying for an extra 30 minutes a day or reviewing one subject before bed.

Hitting those smaller milestones builds momentum, keeps you motivated, and makes your big goal feel achievable. Every small win adds up, making even the most demanding challenges feel doable.

Recognizing and Managing Stress

Stress has a sneaky way of creeping up on you, but once you spot your triggers, you can take control. Maybe it's a packed schedule, a big test coming up, or drama with friends. Whatever it is, recognizing the cause is the first step to handling it like a pro.

For example, if schoolwork stresses you out, create a study schedule that breaks tasks into bite-sized pieces. If you're feeling overwhelmed, take short breaks to recharge.

Once you know what's causing your stress, you can find ways to adapt and stay in control—making tough situations much more manageable.

You Got This!

Life will always have surprises, but with adaptability, resilience, and a positive mindset, you'll be ready for anything. Every challenge is just another chance to grow, learn, and prove to yourself that you can handle whatever comes your way.

Take a deep breath and remember—you're way stronger than you think!

The Build Up

Be Curious

When something new pops up, try looking at it with excitement instead of worry.

- Ask questions
- Explore different possibilities
- Don't rush yourself—figuring things out takes time!

Think about the first time you tried riding a bike. You probably asked for advice, tested different ways to balance, and gave yourself plenty of chances to practice. That curiosity and willingness to learn helped you succeed; the same approach works for anything new life throws your way!

Try New Things

Stepping outside your comfort zone doesn't mean making massive, scary changes—it can be as simple as

- Trying a different way to study
- Learning a new hobby
- Joining a club you've never considered before
- Maybe you volunteer for a class project
- Test out a new sport
- Rearrange your room to see if a fresh setup helps you focus better

These small changes build your adaptability muscle, making it easier to take on bigger challenges in the future.

Focus on Solutions

When things don't go as planned, don't get stuck stressing over the problem—shift your focus to what you can do instead.

Say your group project hits a snag:

- Can you divide the tasks differently or take a new approach?

Or, if your soccer game gets rained out:

- You can practice drills indoors or watch a game to learn new strategies.

Looking for solutions instead of dwelling on setbacks helps you stay flexible, positive, and ready to tackle whatever comes next.

Strengthening Your Resolve

Take Care of Yourself

Being resilient starts with taking care of your body and mind.

- Get enough sleep so you wake up refreshed and ready to go.
- Eat balanced meals that keep your energy up.

And don't forget to unwind!

- Journaling
- Listening to your favorite playlist
- Deep breathing
- Stretching can help you recharge
- A quick walk outside can work wonders!

When you care for yourself, you're setting the foundation for handling challenges with strength and confidence.

Learn from Mistakes

Mistakes aren't failures—they're lessons in disguise.

When something doesn't go as planned, pause and think: "What can I do differently next time?"

Maybe your science project didn't turn out the way you wanted.

Was it because of:

- Time management?
- Teamwork?
- Preparation?

Take what you've learned and use it to improve for next time. The more you reflect and grow, the more confident and capable you'll become.

Lean on Others

You don't have to figure everything out on your own! Friends, family, and teachers are part of your personal support squad and are there to help when needed.

If you're stressed about a big test, talk to a teacher for study tips or vent to a friend. If something's bothering you, sharing your thoughts with someone will make all the difference. Support is always there—you have to reach out for it!

Practice Activity

Think about when you had to deal with a big change or a tough situation.

- How did you handle it?
- What helped you push through?

Write it down or share it with someone. Recognizing your own strengths is the first step toward building them even more!

Key Takeaways

- Adaptability: Stay open to new experiences and adjust to change with a positive attitude.
- Resilience: Bounce back from setbacks and keep moving forward.
- Practical Tips: Be curious, try new things, focus on solutions, care for yourself, learn from mistakes, and ask for help when needed.
- Benefits: These skills help you handle stress, reach your goals, and boost your confidence—making you stronger whenever you face a challenge!

Remember, adaptability and resilience aren't about being perfect. They're about showing up, trying your best, and learning as you go. With these skills in your back pocket, you'll be ready for whatever life throws your way!

6

FINANCIAL LITERACY

> "The goal isn't more money. The goal is living life on your terms."
>
> — CHRIS BROGAN

Money is a part of our daily lives—we earn, spend, and think about it constantly. But the funny thing is that even after years of school prepping us to make a living, many of us never really learn how to manage our money. Instead, we rely on gut instincts, cross our fingers, and hope for the best.

But understanding money is one of the best things you can do for yourself. It's not just about paying bills or stashing cash in a savings account—it's about knowing how money works in every aspect of life.

The sooner you start learning, the more confident and prepared you'll be to tackle life's financial ups and downs. In this chapter, we'll break down the essentials of budgeting, saving, investing, and managing debt while focusing on financial independence.

By the end, you'll truly have the tools and confidence to truly take control of your financial future!

Understanding Money Basics

What is Budgeting?

Budgeting is basically a game plan for your money—it's how you make sure your cash flow is working for you, not just disappearing without a trace. You can even think about it like a treasure map that helps you reach your financial goals without getting lost along the way.

The goal? Make sure you don't blow through your money too fast or come up short before your next paycheck or allowance.

Let's say, for example, you're saving up for a new video game. A solid budget helps you set aside enough while covering the important stuff—like snacks, gas if you drive, or a fun night out with your friends. It's not really about restricting yourself; it's about giving yourself the freedom to enjoy life without stressing over whether you'll have enough left when all the fun dust settles to the ground.

Types of Budgets:

- **Fixed Budgets:** These cover the expenses that stay the same every month, such as your phone bill, gym membership, or subscription service. Since these costs don't change, they're easy to plan for. For instance, if your phone bill is $40 bucks a month, you can budget for it and never have to worry about coming up short. You can think of fixed expenses as the foundation of any budget because they're going to help you organize your money around must-haves.

- **Flexible Budgets:** These are expenses that change from month to month, like grabbing food with friends, shopping, or entertainment. This is the part of your budget that lets you have fun—without going overboard. For example, if you're planning a big weekend outing, you might decide to spend less on snacks that week to make up for it. A flexible budget helps you enjoy life, slay, and remain in control of your financial well-being.

Steps to Create a Budget:

1. Figure Out Your Income

First things first, friends—how much money do you actually have? This includes everything from your allowance and part-time job earnings to birthday cash or side hustles like babysitting or mowing lawns. It's important to count both the steady income and the extra occasional cash so you can have a crystal clear picture of your finances.

2. List Your Expenses

Now that we know what we're working with—write down everything you spend money on. This includes big things such as school supplies and transportation, clothes, or weekend trips, but also all the smaller expenses we don't tend to look at

—like that two-dollar pop you grab every day after school or that iced latte you love on Saturdays.

Even seemingly small expenses can add up fast! Try organizing your list into two categories:

- Essentials (stuff you have to pay for, like bus fare, gas for your car, lunch money, or phone bill).
- Extras (stuff you want, like video games or a new outfit).

Seeing where your money goes helps you figure out which area of your financial life is doing too much and where you can stand to save a few bucks!

3. Set Aside Savings:

Before you start spending, put some money away first. This is the key to making sure you're covered for both big goals and unexpected surprises. Maybe you're saving up for a new game console—setting aside a little each time you get paid helps you get there faster.

But don't forget a backup fund for emergencies, too! A broken phone, for example, or another last-minute expense won't feel like a disaster if you've already saved for it. Try having two separate savings: One for short-term goals and another for long-term needs.

4. Plan for Fun

Budgeting isn't just about responsibilities—you've got to enjoy yourself too! Setting aside money for things like movies, snacks, or outings in general makes sticking to your budget way easier. When you know you've got room for fun, you're less likely to spend impulsively.

Think about what makes you happiest and work it into your budget. You could plan one big treat each month or save a little each week for smaller splurges. Either way, you'll always have something fun to look forward to without messing up your financial goals.

A good budget isn't about limiting yourself! It's about giving yourself more control and freedom. With the right plan in place, you can enjoy your money and make sure you're always prepared for whatever comes next!

Tips for Sticking to a Budget:

Track your spending: I'm sure there's been a time you've had to ask yourself...where's my money gone? Devastating right? The best way to keep ahead of the game is to use an app, a spreadsheet, or even an old-fashioned little notepad to jot down every little expense.

This way, you'll know where you might be overspending and where you can cut back. For finance, swapping out something homemade for a store-bought purchase is a long-game win!

Over time, you will notice a surprisingly decent chunk of money in your savings. Plus, using a tracker for your spending will help you visually understand your money habits so you can strive to make better sense of your relationship with money.

Date	Category	Amount ($)	Payment Method	Notes
2025-03-01	Food	10	Cash	Lunch with friends
2025-03-02	Entertainment	15	Debit Card	Movie ticket
2025-03-03	Transportation	5	Cash	Bus fare
2025-03-04	Shopping	20	Credit Card	New clothes
2025-03-05	Savings	10	Bank Transfer	Saved allowance

Figure 6.1 *A spending tracker spreadsheet that records daily expenses, categorizing spending habits*

Be flexible: Listen, life happens to all of us, and sometimes, your budget needs to adjust. Maybe you had to buy extra school supplies, or your phone died, and there's no saving it. If that's the case, look for areas where you can temporarily cut back—like skipping a gaming subscription or eating out less until you get back on track.

Flexibility also means planning ahead for special occasions. You're more likely to stick with a budget that can adapt to life's ups and downs!

Celebrate Wins!: Sticking to a budget isn't always easy, so when you do it well, go ahead and reward yourself! If you've been consistently saving for a few weeks, treat yourself to something fun, like a new pair of shoes, a book, a game, or just a yummy snack with some friends after school.

These mini rewards keep you motivated and make budgeting feel like a positive habit, not a chore. Hitting milestones, like saving a certain amount or just staying on track for a whole month, makes managing money feel more exciting and keeps you committed to your financial goals.

Saving

Why should you save?

Saving money is one of the best habits you can build—it helps you turn your dreams into reality! Regardless of what you are saving for (college, a car, a game console, etc), setting money aside gives you the power to reach for the stars.

Savings aren't just for the fun stuff; they also act as a safety net. Right now, emergency funds could be simple: the phone needs repair, the bike needs a tire replaced, but learning to do this now will help later on when your expenses and responsibilities have grown as much as you have (buying a home, car maintenance.) The more you save, the more freedom, confidence, and peace of mind you'll have now and in the future.

Types of Savings:

- **Emergency Funds:** Life is full of unexpected surprises, and an emergency fund is there to help you through them. Whether it's covering a sudden expense or helping out when money is tight, having even a small safety net (like $100 to start) can make a huge difference. Over time, aim to save enough to cover 3-6 months of essential expenses—you'll thank yourself later!

- **Goal-Oriented Savings:** These are savings for things you actually want—like concert tickets, a new bike, or a trip with friends. Having a clear goal makes saving feel exciting rather than like a chore. For example, if you want a new pair of sneakers, setting aside $10 a week gets you there faster than you think. The key? Small, steady contributions add up, and having a goal keeps you motivated!

Saving Strategies

Use the 50/30/20 Rule

- A great way to keep your spending balanced is by following the 50/30/20 rule. That means putting 50% of your money toward essentials like school supplies and transportation, 30% toward things you enjoy, like movies or shopping, and 20% straight into savings.
- This method helps you have fun while still making sure you're setting money aside for the future— because saving shouldn't mean missing out on life!

Make Saving Automatic

If you don't have a bank account, you can still set up a foolproof system to save without thinking about it.

- Try using labeled jars or envelopes for different goals —like one for a new bike and another for emergency expenses. Every time you get money, put a set amount into each.
- If you have a digital wallet or bank account, setting up automatic transfers (or getting a parent to help)

ensures you're always putting something away without spending first.

Start Small, Stay Steady

You don't need to stash away huge amounts right away—small steps can lead to big results. Even setting aside just $5 a week adds up to $260 in a year, and that's without counting any extra money you might save along the way.

Watching your savings grow is motivating, and the habit of saving consistently is even more important than the amount itself. The sooner you start, the easier it will be to reach your goals!

Investing

What's the Deal with Investing?

Investing is a way to make your money work for you instead of just sitting there doing nothing or flying out the window. You can think of it as planting a tiny seed that grows into a big, strong tree over time. When you invest, you're buying things—like stocks, bonds, or even real estate—that have the potential to increase in value.

What does this mean? It means your money grows while you do...well, anything else! Even if you're starting, small steps like putting money into savings bonds or index funds can help you build wealth over time.

The best part? Investing early gives your money more time to grow and sets you up for financial freedom down the road.

Types of Investments:

Stocks, Bonds & Mutual Funds

These are some of the most common ways to grow your money:

- **Stocks:** When you buy a stock, you're buying a small piece of a company. If the company does well, your stock value goes up—win! But, if the company struggles...yup, you guessed it, your stock could lose value too.
- **Bonds:** Think of bonds as a loan. You're lending money to a company or the government, and they pay you back with interest. It's a more stable, lower-risk option than stocks.
- **Mutual Funds:** These are like a team effort. Your money gets pooled with other investors' money and is used to buy a mix of stocks, bonds, or other assets. It's a great way to spread out risk while benefiting from professional management.

Each option has its own risk level, so it's important to be mindful and pick an option(s) that fit your goals and comfort zone.

Low-Risk vs. High-Risk Investments

- Low-risk investments (like savings bonds or CDs) are like the slow-and-steady tortoise. They grow gradually and offer security with little chance of loss.
- High-risk investments (like stocks and Cryptocurrency) are more like the hare—potentially fast-growing but also unpredictable. If things go well,

you can definitely make some big gains, but if they don't...you could lose money. Choose wisely!

For beginners, a mix of both can help you find the right balance, but it's best to start small and slow as a teen and save the risk for a little later in life. Either way, it's nice to know you have options and, more importantly, a plan!

Basic Investing Concepts

Diversification: Don't put all Your Eggs in One Basket

One of the smartest moves in investing is spreading your money across different types of assets. Instead of investing everything in one stock, you can mix it up with bonds, mutual funds, or even different industries. This way, if one investment doesn't do well, others might make up for it.

Risk & Reward: Finding the Right Balance

In the investment game, higher risk means higher potential rewards—and losses. For instance, if you invest in a hot new cryptocurrency, you could see some massive gains! But be mindful; there's also a chance it will tank big time! The key here is to figure out how much risk you are comfortable taking and how that aligns (or doesn't) with your long and short-term financial goals.

Inflation: The Sneaky Money Eater

Inflation makes everything more expensive over time, which means your money's buying power shrinks. Let's look closer: if you buy a ten-dollar meal at your favorite fast-food spot today, the same meal could cost twelve or maybe fifteen bucks in a few years, depending on the fluctuations of the economy.

What does that have to do with your savings?

I'm glad you asked because if you keep your money just sitting around (doing nothing) in a regular savings account, it won't keep up with inflation. That's why investing in things that will grow faster than inflation (stocks or index funds) is so important—it keeps your money from losing value over time!

Investing in Index Funds

Being new to the world of investing, it's valuable to know that index funds are your friends! They are absolutely one of the best ways to start! Instead of picking individual stocks, an index fund lets you invest in a bunch of companies at once, reducing the risk while still giving you solid growth.

Why Index Funds Rock:

- They automatically spread out your investment
- They're lower risk compared to individual socks.
- They've historically shown steady, long-term growth.
- They're super easy to manage—no stock-picking stress!

Some beginner-friendly index funds include:

- Vanguard S&P ETF (VOO): Tracks S&P 500 for long-term growth.
- Vanguard Health Care Index Fund ETF (VHT): It focuses on healthcare companies, which are a stable and growing industry.

- Schwab U.S. Dividend Equity ETF (SCHD): Invests in companies with a strong track record of paying dividends.
- Consumer Staples Select Sector SPDR Fund (XLP): This fund includes some big-name companies that produce everyday essentials.
- Fidelity ZERO Large Cap Index Fund (FNILX): A no-fee option that tracks large U.S. companies.
- SPDR S&P 500 ETF Trust (SPY): One of the oldest and most popular index funds.

These funds are super friendly for beginners, affordable, and a great way to grow your money over time without having to constantly be stalking the stock market—who has that kind of time?

Managing Debt

Good Debt: Your Money's Working for You

Good debt is the kind that helps you build a better future. It's like borrowing money with a game plan—one that leads to more financial stability down the road. Think about student loans: Sure, they're a pain now, but they can open doors to higher-paying jobs.

Or a small business loan—risky, but if it helps you build something profitable, it's worth it. Good debt usually has lower interest rates and is tied to something that grows in value or makes you money.

The key? Use it wisely, and make sure you can pay it back!

A mortgage is another great example of 'good debt.' While buying a home requires a big financial commitment, real estate typically appreciates over time, making homeownership a solid long-term investment. Even taking out a loan to improve your skills---such as professional certifications---can be a smart move. The trick here is to borrow responsibly and do everything you can to keep interest rates in check (like paying your bills on time!), ensuring that your good debt is helping you move forward financially.

Bad Debt: The Budget Buster

Bad debt, on the other hand, is like inviting financial stress into your life. It usually means borrowing money for things that don't hold value or boost your future. Credit card debt is a classic example—especially when it's racked up on impulse buys (looking at you, latest gadgets and online shopping sprees). High interest rates can make it tough to escape the cycle, turning what seemed like a fun purchase into a long-term financial headache. Instead of helping you build wealth, bad debt drains your wallet and makes it harder to save or invest.

It's important, as always, to be mindful of that!

We all love nice things, and there's nothing wrong with that! But taking out an auto loan for luxury cars you can't afford is not a great step toward having a secure financial future! Pay day loans with sky-high interest and financing expensive vacations are also a couple of examples of the ways debt could negatively affect you.

These purchases might indeed bring you temporary satisfaction. Still, they will not contribute long-term to your financial wellness of the future and will not offer the stability you want.

The key to avoiding bad debt? Live within your means, budget wisely, and focus on borrowing only when it truly benefits your future.

Wait... Can Good Debt Turn Bad?

Absolutely! Just because a type of debt is usually considered "good" doesn't mean it always is. Take student loans, for example. They're supposed to be an investment in your future, but paying them back can be a struggle if you borrow a ton for a degree with limited job prospects.

If your passion isn't a high-paying field, that's okay! But it's worth thinking about how you fund it—maybe by saving up beforehand or working to cover costs instead of taking on massive debt.

An intelligent approach now can save you from financial stress later!

Borrowing Wisely & Paying Smart

Only borrow when necessary. Ask yourself: Will this debt help me in the long run? Emergencies, education, or starting a business? Maybe. A vacation you can't afford? Probably not. Having a realistic repayment plan is key!

Pay on time, always. Late payments mean extra fees and higher interest rates, which make debt even harder to manage. Set reminders, automate payments—whatever works to keep you on track. Plus, a good payment history boosts your credit score!

Debt Management Tips

Prioritize High-Interest Debt

Credit cards and payday loans? Get those out of the way first! The higher the interest rate, the more money you lose over time. Knocking out high-interest debt first saves you serious cash and stress.

Snowball Method: Pay off the smallest debts first for quick wins and motivation. Great for staying pumped about progress!

Avalanche Method: Focus on debts with the highest interest rates first. It saves more money in the long run.

Both work—go with whatever keeps you motivated!

Avoid New Debt While Paying Off Old Debt

If you're already juggling loans or credit card balances, hold off on taking on more. More debt = more stress and less flexibility with your money. Knock out what you owe first, then think about new financial commitments.

The Freedom of Financial Independence

What is Financial Independence?

It's the ability to make life choices without money being the main barrier. When you're financially independent, you can chase your goals—whether that's traveling, starting a business, or just having peace of mind—without constantly stressing over cash.

Steps Toward Independence

- Build good money habits early. Budget, save, and invest wisely.

- Have an emergency fund. Even a tiny cushion makes a big difference when life throws surprises your way.

- Live within your means. Spend less than you earn—it's simple but powerful.

- Invest! Grow your money over time with smart investments (while understanding the risks).

Hands-On Finance: Let's Practice!

Creating a Budget

Activity: Plan a monthly budget with a pretend income of $300. Divide it using the 50/30/20 rule:

- Needs (50%): School supplies, transportation ($150)

- Wants (30%): Fun stuff like gaming, movies ($90)

- Savings (20%): Emergency fund, future goals ($60)

Now, adjust it when unexpected costs pop up—because they always do!

Tracking Expenses

Activity: For one week, write down every expense (snacks, rides, subscriptions—you name it). Sort them into categories: essentials, wants, and impulse buys.

Reflection: Are you overspending in one area? Maybe vending machine snacks are adding up more than you thought! Adjust your habits and watch the savings grow.

Mock Investment Game

Activity: Pretend to invest $1,000 in stocks, bonds, and mutual funds. Divide it based on your risk tolerance—maybe $500 in stocks for growth, $300 in bonds for stability, and $200 in mutual funds for balance. Check how market changes affect your choices.

Want to try this for real? Search for online mock investment tools to practice without actual money. It's a risk-free way to learn how investing works!

Building an Emergency Fund

- Set a goal—like saving $500 in a year.

- Add small amounts regularly, like $10 a week.

- Find an accountability partner to help you stay on track!

Having savings ready for emergencies keeps you from relying on credit cards or loans when unexpected expenses hit.

Key Takeaways

- Budgeting = Smart Money Moves. Knowing where your money goes keeps spending in check.
- Savings Matter. Even small amounts add up—especially for emergencies!

- Investing Grows Your Wealth. Even simple investments can build long-term financial security.
- Debt Can Be Managed. Learn to tell good from bad and pay off debt wisely.
- Financial Independence = Freedom. Good money habits now mean fewer worries and more options later.

Taking control of your finances today sets you up for success tomorrow! Start small, stay consistent, and enjoy the journey to financial freedom.

7

TIME MANAGEMENT

"There is never enough time to do everything, but there is always enough time to do the most important thing."

— BRIAN TRACY

Time management isn't just about cramming every task humanly possible into your day—it's more about making space for the activities and responsibilities that truly matter. We can be talking about crushing your goals, staying on top of schoolwork, or just having enough time to relax and do whatever makes your heart space sing; mastering your schedule can make life much more manageable and less stressful!

Think of time as your most valuable currency—you can't save it up or get it back once it's spent, so using it wisely is key. The best part about this? You are the boss of your time!

This chapter is packed with simple hacks, powerful tools, and fun activities to help you take control of your day, boost your productivity, and still have plenty of time to chill. We have a lot to unpack, so let's jump in!

Managing Your Day

Turning Overwhelm into Action: The Power of SMART Goals

We have all been there—staring at a long to-do list, feeling completely overwhelmed, and not knowing where to start. It's frustrating, stressful, and, let's be honest, the procrastination feels good...until it doesn't.

Think of goals like a roadmap that helps you navigate your day, week..., and month! This is the game changer that's going to give you the direction you need and help you focus on what matters.

But here is the catch: not all goals are created equal. Some goals are too fuzzy to be useful, and some can be way too big, letting us get carried away with ourselves.

Enter SMART Goals, the secret weapon you didn't know you needed. These are exactly like their name suggests: designed to keep you focused, organized, and —most importantly—help you accomplish what you set out to do!

Let's say your goal is to boost your grades. You could master a new study technique like learning to take killer notes, or perhaps you'd really like to become a better basketball player or musician.

No matter what it is, the concept of SMART Goals will give you a clear and structured plan to follow.

What Are SMART Goals?

Let's break it down!

SMART goals are about setting clear, realistic, and trackable objectives that make achieving success easier.

The term SMART stands for:

Specific – Be clear about what you want.

Measurable – Find a way to track your progress.

Achievable – Set a goal that challenges you but is still possible.

Realistic – Make sure it fits into your life without overwhelming you.

Time-bound – Set a deadline to keep yourself accountable.

By following these five principles, you'll break big goals into smaller, manageable steps that keep you motivated and on track. No more setting unrealistic goals and then giving up because they feel impossible!

Breaking Down SMART Goals

1. Specific: Be Clear About What You Want

A goal should never be vague. Saying, "I want to get better at math," sounds nice, but it doesn't tell you what to do or where to start. A specific goal would be:

"I will complete five practice problems from my math workbook every day."

This way, you know exactly what you need to do, making

taking action easier. The more detailed your goal, the easier it is to follow through.

Tip: If your goal feels unclear, ask yourself: What exactly do I want to accomplish? How will I do it? Why is it important? Answering these questions will help you refine your goal.

2. Measurable: Track Your Progress

How do you know if you're getting closer to your goal? You measure it! Adding numbers or specific milestones makes progress more visible.

Instead of saying, "I want to read more," try:

"I will read 20 pages every evening before bed."

This way, you can track your success and adjust if needed. Seeing progress (even small wins) keeps you motivated and moving forward.

Tip: Use a checklist, a journal, or an app to keep track of your progress. Seeing your accomplishments laid out in front of you can be a huge confidence booster!

3. Achievable: Set Goals You Can Actually Reach

It's great to challenge yourself, but you might get discouraged and give up if your goal is too extreme. Goals should push you to grow while being realistic about where you are now.

For example, if you struggle with math, saying, "I'll master calculus in two weeks" is probably unrealistic. But saying:

"I will master one new math concept each week by practicing 30 minutes daily."

It is challenging yet doable!

Tip: If your goal feels too big, break it down into smaller steps. Instead of "write a novel," start with "write 500 words a day." Small steps lead to big wins!

4. Realistic: Fit Goals Into Your Life

Just because something is achievable doesn't mean it's realistic for your life. If you already have school, sports, and other commitments, setting a goal to practice guitar for four hours a day might not make sense.

A realistic goal takes into account your schedule and energy levels. Instead of:

"I'll practice basketball for 3 hours every day,"

Try:

"I'll practice basketball for 45 minutes after school, Monday to Friday."

This way, you're still making progress without overwhelming yourself or burning out.

Tip: Ask yourself: Do I have the time, energy, and resources to commit to this goal? If not, adjust it until it fits into your lifestyle.

5. Time-Bound: Set a Deadline

Without a deadline, a goal can drag on forever. A time-bound goal adds a sense of urgency and helps you stay committed.

Instead of:

"I'll finish my science project someday,"

Try:

"I will complete my science project by Friday at 5 PM."

A clear deadline helps you prioritize your time and avoid last-minute panic. It also gives you something to work toward, which keeps motivation high!

Tip: Break long-term goals into smaller deadlines

Why SMART Goals Work

The magic of SMART goals is that they turn overwhelming ideas into clear action plans. Instead of feeling stuck, you have a step-by-step guide to follow. Plus, they:

- Keep you motivated by showing progress.
- Prevent frustration by making goals realistic and achievable.
- Help you manage your time effectively.
- Make big dreams feel manageable and doable.

So next time you're setting a goal—whether for school, a personal project, or self-improvement—use the SMART method to ensure it's clear, actionable, and set up for success!

Overcoming Procrastination and Prioritizing Tasks

Procrastination: Why We Do It and How to Beat It

Let's be real—procrastination is something we've all fallen victim to at some point. You sit down to start an assignment, and suddenly, your brain convinces you that now is the perfect time to clean your entire room, check social media, or watch just one episode of your favorite show.

Before you know it, hours have passed, and the thing you were supposed to do is still untouched. Sound familiar?

Procrastination happens when we delay tasks, even when we know they're important. It's often fueled by fear, uncertainty, or the simple fact that distractions are way more fun.

Maybe you're avoiding a project because you're afraid of not doing it well, or the instructions seem confusing, so you don't even know where to start. And let's be honest—sometimes watching videos or playing games sounds a whole lot better than tackling a long list of to-dos.

The Good News?

Procrastination isn't a life sentence. Once you understand why it happens, you can take steps to break the cycle and get things done without the stress of last-minute panic. Let's dive into some simple, effective ways to beat procrastination and enjoy the feeling of productivity.

How to Beat Procrastination

1. Break Tasks into Smaller Steps: Big tasks can feel overwhelming, making it easy to avoid them altogether. The trick is to break them down into smaller, manageable pieces. Instead of saying, "I need to finish my entire history project," try breaking it into bite-sized steps:

- Find three good sources for research.
- Write a rough outline.
- Draft the introduction.
- Complete one section at a time.

Each small step makes the task feel less intimidating, and every time you check something off your list, you'll feel a little burst of accomplishment. Plus, starting is the hardest part—once you begin, you'll likely find that momentum carries you forward.

2. The 2-Minute Rule: If something takes less than two minutes, do it immediately. This simple rule prevents tiny tasks from piling up and becoming overwhelming. Examples include:

- Replying to a quick email
- Throwing away that empty snack bag on your desk
- Putting your shoes away instead of leaving them in the middle of the floor

Taking care of small things right away clears up mental space and helps you stay on top of your to-do list with minimal effort.

3. Make It Fun: Reward Yourself!

Hard work doesn't have to feel like punishment. In fact, rewarding yourself after completing a difficult task can train your brain to associate productivity with positive feelings.

Here's how you can do it:

- Finish your assignment? Treat yourself to an episode of your favorite show.
- Knocked out an hour of studying? Take a snack break or go for a quick walk.
- Wrote a killer essay? Reward yourself with 20 minutes of gaming or scrolling TikTok guilt-free.

These little rewards keep motivation high and make even the most tedious tasks feel a little less painful.

Prioritizing Tasks: What Needs to Be Done Right Now?

Sometimes, the hardest part of getting things done is figuring out where to start. Prioritizing your tasks helps you focus on what matters most and stops you from wasting time on things that don't move you forward.

One of the best ways to prioritize is using the Eisenhower Matrix—a super simple method that helps you separate what's urgent from what's actually important.

The Eisenhower Matrix Breakdown:

EISENHOWER MATRIX

	IMPORTANT	NOT IMPORTANT
URGENT	DO THESE IMMEDIATELY	DELEGATE OR DEFER
NOT URGENT	SCHEDULE AND PLAN AHEAD	ELIMINATE OR LIMIT

Figure 7.1 *Eisenhower Matrix helps prioritize tasks by urgency and importance.*

Urgent & Important: Do these FIRST! These tasks have tight deadlines and serious consequences if ignored. Example:

Studying for a test tomorrow or finishing an assignment due tonight. Knock these out early so you're not scrambling at the last minute.

Important but Not Urgent: Schedule these. These tasks matter in the long run but don't need to be done right now. Example: Working on a project that's due in two weeks or prepping for a future exam. If you plan ahead, you can complete them stress-free.

Urgent but Not Important: Delegate these when possible. These tasks feel pressing but aren't crucial for your success. Example: Answering non-essential emails or running errands for someone else. If you can, let someone else handle them!

Neither Urgent nor Important: Cut these out! These are the distractions that waste your time without benefiting you. Example: Mindlessly scrolling social media or re-organizing your desk again. These activities aren't bad, but if they stop you from getting real work done, they must go.

Additional Procrastination-Busting Tips

Set Time Limits: Use a timer to work in short, focused bursts (like the Pomodoro Technique—25 minutes of work, 5-minute break). This keeps you focused and prevents burnout.

Plan Ahead: Write a to-do list the night before so you wake up with a game plan. Bonus points if you prioritize the hardest task first!

Create a Distraction-Free Zone: Put your phone on Do Not Disturb, block distracting websites, or work in a quiet space to avoid getting sidetracked.

Find an Accountability Partner: Having someone check in on your progress (or working alongside a friend) can keep you motivated and on track.

Procrastination might be sneaky, but with the right strategies, you can outsmart it. The key is to start small, stay consistent, and make work feel rewarding instead of overwhelming. Remember, productivity isn't about working non-stop—it's about working smarter, so you have more time to enjoy the things you love.

So, next time you catch yourself avoiding a task, try one of these techniques and see how much easier it gets. You've got this!

Tools and Techniques

Tools and Techniques: Making Time Management Fun and Easy

Managing your time isn't just about making to-do lists and hoping for the best—it's about using the right tools and techniques to stay on track without feeling overwhelmed.

Let's be real: staying organized doesn't come naturally to everyone (hello, procrastination!), but the good news is, there are tons of ways to make it easier. If you're a planner who loves physically checking off tasks or needs digital reminders to stay on top of things, there's a tool out there that's perfect for you.

This section is all about helping you find the best methods to manage your time—without feeling like you're drowning in responsibilities.

Planners and Productivity Apps: Your Secret Weapons for Staying on Track

Planners and productivity apps are total game-changers when it comes to getting stuff done. Think of them as your personal assistant—except you don't have to pay them, and they never take a day off.

They help you organize your tasks, remind you of important deadlines, and keep you from double-booking yourself (because we've all accidentally promised to be in two places at once).

Some people love the old-school vibe of a physical planner—writing things down, decorating with colorful pens, and experiencing the deep satisfaction of crossing off completed tasks. Others prefer the ease of digital tools that sync across all devices, send reminders, and let you edit things on the go.

No matter your style, there's a perfect option for you.

Popular Productivity Tools to Check Out:

- Trello or Asana – Perfect for organizing tasks, setting deadlines, and tracking progress. Great for visual thinkers!
- Google Calendar – The ultimate scheduling tool for keeping track of appointments, deadlines, and events all in one place. Bonus: you can set reminders so you never forget an important date!
- Notion – A super flexible app for planning, note-taking, and organizing your life. Whether you're tracking goals, making to-do lists, or keeping a journal, Notion can do it all.
- Forest App – Struggle with distractions? This app helps you stay focused by growing a virtual tree when

you avoid using your phone. If you exit early, your tree dies. It's oddly motivating!

How to Choose the Right Tool:

- Love writing things down? A physical planner is your best bet. It's perfect if you enjoy the satisfaction of physically checking off tasks or doodling in the margins while brainstorming.
- Always on your phone or laptop? A digital app is the way to go. You'll love being able to set reminders, sync across multiple devices, and quickly update your plans on the fly.
- Need motivation? Try an app that gamifies productivity, like Habitica or the Forest app. These turn productivity into a game, making time management more fun.

The key is experimenting with different tools until you find what works best for your lifestyle. You might even discover that a combination of both digital and physical planning keeps you on track.

Time Management Hacks: Work Smarter, Not Harder

If you've ever wished there were a way to get more done in less time (without feeling totally drained), time management hacks are the answer. These simple techniques help you work efficiently, avoid distractions, and finish tasks instead of just thinking about them.

The Pomodoro Technique: Beat Procrastination One Timer at a Time

The Pomodoro Technique is a simple yet powerful way to stay focused while avoiding burnout. It's based on the idea that working in short, intense bursts followed by breaks keeps your brain fresh and productive.

Here's how it works:

Pick a task you need to work on.

- Set a timer for 25 minutes and work without distractions. (Yes, that means no checking your phone!)
- When the timer rings, take a 5-minute break—stretch, grab a snack, or relax.
- Repeat this cycle four times, then take a longer break (15–30 minutes).

Why does this method work? Because it helps you stay focused without feeling like you're stuck working for hours on end. You're training your brain to stay engaged while also giving it the breaks it needs to recharge.

It's a little like turning productivity into a game—and who doesn't love winning?

The "Eat the Frog" Method: Get the Hardest Task Done First

This oddly named technique is based on a quote from Mark Twain: "If it's your job to eat a frog, it's best to do it first thing in the morning. And if it's your job to eat two frogs, it's best to eat the biggest one first." Translation? Tackle your hardest, most important task before distractions and procrastination take over.

If you keep putting off a challenging project, an annoying email, or a big assignment, just get it out of the way first. Once it's done, the rest of your day feels easier. Plus, you'll feel super accomplished before lunch!

The 80/20 Rule: Focus on What Really Matters

Not all tasks are created equal. The 80/20 Rule (a.k.a. the Pareto Principle) suggests that 80% of your results come from just 20% of your efforts. In other words, a small handful of tasks will have the biggest impact. Instead of wasting time on busy work, identify the tasks that will make the most difference and prioritize those.

Ask yourself:

- Which tasks will help me the most in the long run?
- What's important, and what's just "busy work" that doesn't really matter?
- Am I spending too much time on low-value activities instead of focusing on what moves the needle?

By applying the 80/20 Rule, you can eliminate unnecessary work and focus on what truly matters—helping you get more done in less time.

Managing your time doesn't have to be stressful or boring. With the right tools, a few simple hacks, and a little self-awareness, you can take control of your schedule, avoid procrastination, and enjoy the process.

The goal is to make your time work for you!

POMODORO TECHNIQUE

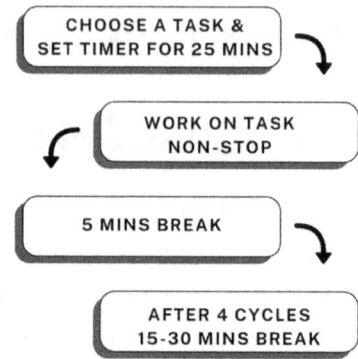

Figure 7.2 Work in focused intervals, followed by short breaks, to boost productivity and maintain focus.

Time Blocking & Task Batching: Master Your Schedule!

Sometimes, the to-do list feels never-ending, and somehow, it never seems like there's enough time in the day!

You're not alone on that!

But don't worry—you can regain control of your time without feeling overwhelmed.

Enter time blocking and task batching, two super simple but incredibly effective techniques that help you stay organized, focused, and way less stressed.

Time Blocking: Give Every Task Its Own VIP Slot

Think of time blocking, like making a reservation for your tasks. Instead of just hoping you'll get around to everything (and then realizing it's bedtime and you forgot half your to-dos), this method helps you assign specific time slots for different activities. It's like meal-prepping for your schedule—you know exactly what's coming and when.

How It Works:

Instead of saying, "I'll do my homework later," you set a specific time:

- 4:00–5:00 PM → Homework
- 5:00–5:30 PM → Exercise
- 5:30–6:00 PM → Chill time (yes, relaxing deserves a time block too!)

By planning out your day like this, you avoid the dreaded "What should I do next?" decision fatigue.

It helps you stay focused because you know what you should be doing at any moment.

And guess what? You don't have to be super rigid about it—life happens! Time blocking is about creating structure, not stress. If things shift a little, that's totally okay. The goal is to have a plan that keeps you moving forward.

Task Batching: Work Smarter, Not Harder

What's Task Batching?

It's when you group similar tasks instead of constantly switching between different activities. This helps you:

- Save time by eliminating the mental effort of switching gears.
- Stay focused because your brain stays in the same "mode."

- Feel less exhausted at the end of the day.

Examples of Task Batching in Action:

Homework Mode: Instead of doing a math problem, texting a friend, writing an essay, and checking Instagram, batch your assignments together. Finish all your schoolwork first, then take a well-earned break!

Chore Power Hour: Instead of randomly cleaning one thing during the day, set a 30-minute block to knock out ALL your chores at once. Laundry? Dishes? Vacuuming? Boom—done.

Inbox Zero: Instead of checking emails or messages every 10 minutes, set aside a specific time to go through all of them in one go. No more getting sidetracked by notifications!

Organizing your tasks this way creates a smoother workflow, feels more accomplished, and frees up extra time for the fun stuff. Win-win!

Practice: Try These Fun Time-Management Challenges!

Okay, now that you know the techniques, it's time to put them into action. These activities will help you see where your time goes and figure out how to make the most of it.

Activity 1: The Time-Tracking Challenge

Where does all your time go? Let's find out!

Goal: Discover how you're currently spending your time so you can make better choices.

How to Do It:

Write down everything you do for one day (or a full week if you're feeling ambitious). Yes, everything—from studying to scrolling TikTok.

Sort your activities into categories (e.g., school, hobbies, chores, screen time).

Calculate how much time you spend on each category.

Reflection Questions:

- Were you surprised by how much time you spent on certain activities?
- What's one small change you could make to use your time better?
- Is there anything you wish you had spent more or less time on?

Activity 2: Create Your Ideal Daily Schedule

Now that you've tracked your time let's build a daily routine that actually works for you.

Goal: Plan your day in a way that balances school, personal time, and fun!

How to Do It:

- Grab a blank planner, piece of paper, or even your phone's notes app.
- Map out your day, making sure to include school, homework, hobbies, exercise, and relaxation.
- Adjust your schedule to match your priorities—if something's important, give it the time it deserves!

Reflection Questions:

- What worked well this week?
- What was the most challenging part of sticking to a schedule?
- What's one thing you're proud of accomplishing?

You're in Control of Your Time!

Managing your time isn't about being perfect—it's about making small, smart choices that help you get more done without feeling overwhelmed. Whether you're using time blocking to stay organized, task batching to work more efficiently, or tracking your habits to find a better balance, you're building skills that will help you for life.

Once you start using these techniques, you'll free up more time for the things you *actually* enjoy. Because let's be honest—more time for fun, hobbies, and relaxation? Yes, please!

So go ahead, give these strategies a try, and take charge of your schedule!

Key Takeaways

- **SMART Goals**: Clear, specific goals help you focus and achieve more.
- **Beating Procrastination**: Breaking tasks into smaller steps and rewarding yourself makes tackling them easier.
- **Planners and Apps**: Find tools that fit your style to stay organized.
- **Time Management Techniques**: Stay productive by using strategies like Pomodoro, time blocking, and

task batching.

- **Track Your Time**: Understanding how you spend your time helps you improve and reach your goals.

8

BUILDING CONNECTIONS
(NETWORKING)

 "Building relationships is not about transactions –
it's about connections."

— MICHELLE TILLIS LEDERMAN

If someone asked me to name the top three skills that can impact a person's success, networking would absolutely make the list. And no, I'm not talking about awkward small talk at events or stuffing your pockets with flyers you'll never look at again.

Real networking is so much more than that.

At its core, networking is about building real relationships with people who can inspire, guide, and support you—and whom you can help in return. It could be finding a mentor, discovering new opportunities, or just making new friends; networking can help you learn and grow in ways you might never expect.

It's not about collecting contacts or trying to impress people but about creating meaningful connections that can enrich your life in countless ways.

In this chapter, we will break down what networking means and uncover some of the best ways to build and maintain your network.

And, it doesn't matter if you're a natural social butterfly or someone who'd rather avoid networking altogether, don't worry—I've got tips and tricks that will make the process feel easy, natural, and even fun.

What is Networking, Really?

Networking is all about connecting with others and building relationships that help everyone grow. Many people think it's just about knowing as many people as possible, but in reality, it's about fostering genuine, meaningful connections. These relationships aren't just beneficial in the present—they can support you, guide you, and even open doors to opportunities in the future.

There are two main types of networks:

1. Personal Networks

Your network includes family, friends, classmates, teachers, and mentors—the people who already know you and want to see you succeed. These relationships form the foundation of your network, providing a safe space for growth, learning, and support.

For instance:

- A teacher might help you choose a career path.
- A mentor could teach you a new skill or introduce you to someone influential in your field.
- A close friend might recommend you for an opportunity you didn't even know existed.

Even though these relationships often form naturally, strengthening them takes effort. Stay in touch, show appreciation, and be there for the people in your network. Because of these connections, you never know when an opportunity will come your way!

2. Professional Networks

Your professional network includes connections related to careers or shared interests, such as coworkers, professionals, members of online communities, or even guest speakers you've met at a school event.

Professional networks are a goldmine of opportunities, from discovering internships to gaining firsthand knowledge about a career path.

For example:

- You might connect with someone at an event who later becomes your mentor.
- An online community could introduce you to people who share your passions and help you grow in your field of interest.
- A former coworker might recommend you for a promotion.

Networking isn't just for getting something—it's a two-way street. Offer help, share knowledge, and be supportive. Relationships built on trust and mutual benefit are the ones that last and truly make a difference in your life.

How to Build and Maintain Your Network

Building a strong network doesn't happen overnight, and it might seem intimidating if you don't know where to start. The good news is, it's easier than you think. Here's how to begin:

1. Start with Whom You Know

You don't have to start from scratch. Your network already exists—you just need to recognize and nurture it. Talk to your friends, family, teachers, and colleagues. Let them know your interests and goals. You never know who might be able to help or introduce you to someone valuable.

2. Be Genuine and Curious

People can tell when you're only reaching out because you want something. Instead, focus on building real relationships by being genuinely interested in others. Ask about their work, their passions, and their experiences. Listen more than you speak. Show enthusiasm and curiosity—people love sharing their knowledge with someone who truly cares.

3. Attend Events and Get Involved

Networking events aren't just for professionals in suits. Look for events that align with your interests, such as:

- Career fairs
- Industry meetups

- Workshops and conferences
- Online webinars and virtual networking sessions
- Join clubs, volunteer groups, or online communities related to your field.

Getting involved in these spaces will naturally connect you with like-minded people and help you grow your network effortlessly.

4. Use Social Media Wisely

If used correctly, platforms like LinkedIn, X, and even Instagram can be powerful networking tools. Connect with people, engage with their content, and participate in discussions.

When reaching out to someone new, personalize your message instead of just hitting "connect" without context. Mention a shared interest or why you admire their work—it makes a huge difference.

5. Follow Up and Stay in Touch

Meeting someone once isn't enough—you have to nurture the relationship. Send a quick message after an event, comment on their posts, or check in occasionally. A simple "Hey, I saw this article and thought of you!" can go a long way in keeping connections alive.

6. Offer Value

One of the best ways to strengthen your network is by being helpful. Share resources, introduce people, and support others whenever you can. Networking isn't just about what you can get—it's also about what you can give. The more you help others, the more they'll want to help you in return.

7. Don't Be Afraid to Ask

Don't hesitate to ask if you need advice, guidance, or an introduction. Most people enjoy helping others, especially if they see that you're genuinely passionate and hardworking. The key is to be polite, direct, and appreciative. Even if they can't help right now, they might in the future.

Overcoming Networking Anxiety

Not everyone feels comfortable networking, and that's okay. If you're shy or introverted, try these tips:

Start small: Start with people you know and gradually expand your network.

Prepare in advance: Have a few questions or topics in mind before attending events.

Use online networking: Engaging with people online can be less intimidating than in-person interactions.

Remember, people want to connect: Most people are open to networking and happy to have a conversation.

The Power of Networking

Building a strong network takes time, effort, and a willingness to step outside your comfort zone. But the rewards? They're endless.

Your network can help you grow, open doors to opportunities, and provide support in ways you never imagined. It could be finding a mentor, landing your dream job, or simply learning from inspiring people; networking has the power to change your life!

So start today! Reach out, make connections, and invest in relationships that matter. Because when you surround yourself with the right people, the possibilities are limitless.

How to Build a Network (Without It Feeling Like a Chore!)

Let's be real—networking can sound super formal and intimidating, but it's just about connecting with people who share your interests. Spoiler alert: You're probably already doing it without even realizing it!

Here's how to build a solid network in a way that feels natural, fun, and totally not awkward.

Start with Your Inner Circle

Before you start stressing about networking events or reaching out to strangers, look at the people already in your life—your family, friends, classmates, teachers, coaches, and even that super-friendly barista you always chat with. These people already support and encourage you, making them the perfect starting point.

Share your interests with them and see if they know someone who might be a great connection. If they do, don't be shy—ask if they can introduce you! Networking through mutual acquaintances is one of the easiest (and least nerve-wracking) ways to grow your circle.

Go Where the People Are (a.k.a. Events!)

There's no better way to meet like-minded folks than by showing up at places where they hang out. Think workshops, school clubs, community events, career fairs, or even hobby-based meetups.

For example, if you're into art, check out a local gallery opening or join a painting class. Love science? Hit up a STEM fair or join a robotics club. The more you put yourself out there, the more opportunities you'll find to meet people who get excited about the same things you do.

Join Online Communities (Because the Internet is Magic)

Not a fan of in-person events? No problem! The internet is full of people who love what you love. Join forums, Facebook groups, Discord servers, or Reddit threads related to your hobbies or career goals.

If you're into gaming, find a community around your favorite game. Love photography? Share your work in a group where others can give feedback and inspiration. Into coding? Try participating in an online hackathon.

These spaces are goldmines for meeting people with shared interests, learning new things, and even discovering potential mentors.

How to Maintain Your Network (Without Being That Person Who Only Reaches Out When They Need Something)

Keeping those connections strong once you've built a network is just as important. Here's how to nurture your relationships without it feeling forced or transactional.

Stay in Touch (It's Easier Than You Think!)

You don't have to send long, formal emails to stay connected. A simple text, DM, or quick check-in like, "Hey! Saw this article and thought of you," works wonders. Even a casual "Hope you're doing well!" message can keep the connection warm.

If you're feeling bold, set up a coffee catch-up or a quick Zoom call to chat.

Celebrate Wins (Because Everyone Loves a Hype Friend)

Did someone in your network land a new job, win an award, or finish a big project? Send them a quick congrats! A simple, "Wow, that's awesome! So happy for you!" shows you genuinely care about their success. Little things like this make you a memorable and valued connection.

Be Someone People Can Count On

If you say you'll do something, follow through. Whether it's showing up on time, helping a friend with a project, or keeping a promise, being reliable builds trust. And trust? That's the secret sauce to strong, lasting connections. When people know they can count on you, they're more likely to return the favor and think of you for future opportunities.

Overcoming Shyness & Making Meaningful Connections

If the thought of networking makes you want to curl up under a blanket and never leave your house, don't worry—you're not alone. Even the most confident people feel awkward sometimes. The good news? You don't need to be the loudest person in the room to build great connections.

Why Do We Get Shy?

Shyness often comes from overthinking—worrying about what people will think, fearing rejection, or stressing about saying the "wrong" thing. But here's the truth: most people are too busy worrying about themselves to scrutinize your every word. The more you practice putting yourself out there, the easier it gets!

Tips to Overcome Shyness & Connect with Confidence

Practice Your Introductions – It helps to have a go-to way to introduce yourself. Try: "Hey, I'm [Name], and I'm super into [hobby/career]. What about you?" Practicing with friends or even in front of the mirror can make it feel more natural.

Start Small – One-on-one conversations are way less intimidating than big groups. Instead of trying to work the whole room at an event, start by chatting with one person at a time.

Ask Open-Ended Questions – People love talking about themselves! Try questions like, "What got you into [their interest]?" or "What's the coolest thing you've learned lately?" These keep the conversation flowing and take the pressure off you to do all the talking.

Networking is Just Making Friends with a Purpose

At the end of the day, networking isn't about collecting business cards or adding random LinkedIn connections. It's about forming real relationships with people who share your interests and can help you grow. And who knows? The people you connect with today might become future collaborators, mentors, or lifelong friends. So put yourself out there, be yourself, and have fun with it!

Making Connections That Matter

Connecting with people on a deeper level is way more impactful than just knowing a lot of people casually. It's important to remember that networking isn't just for adults in suits! It's your ticket to incredible opportunities, friendships, and experiences. Just as you would level up in a game, each connection unlocks potential quests, skills, and allies for your journey.

To make meaningful connections:

- Be genuinely interested in others.
- Listen actively,
- Ask thoughtful questions
- Remember little things about them.

Let me give you an example: if someone mentions they love hiking, ask about their favorite trails next time you chat or share a hiking spot you think they'd enjoy. It shows that you care about their interests, and that goes a long way in strengthening bonds and building lasting relationships.

Broaden Your Knowledge to Contribute

Want to stand out in conversations?

Get a little more knowledgeable about a variety of topics. Reading up on different subjects helps you keep up with discussions and contributes in a way that makes you sound informed and approachable.

Learning about tech trends, social issues, or even pop culture can give you great talking points for both formal and casual chats. Plus, it shows you're curious and open-minded—qualities that help you connect with others!

Tips for Broadening Your Knowledge

- **Read Widely:** Dive into books, articles, and blogs that pique your interest. Mix it up with stuff that challenges you to think differently.
- **Watch Documentaries or Educational Videos:** Platforms like YouTube or Netflix have amazing resources on everything from history to science. Short docs can offer quick insights, while series lets you dive deeper.
- **Join Discussion Groups:** Get involved in book clubs, online forums, or community chats. Hearing different perspectives will keep you learning and motivated.
- **Stay Updated on Current Events:** Follow the news so you're in the loop. Being informed makes you relatable and lets you contribute valuable insights.
- **Experiment with New Hobbies:** Whether it's photography, gardening, or coding, trying new things gives you new skills and opens up fun conversations with others who share those interests.

Real-World Networking

Networking in the real world is all about turning what you've learned into action. Whether it's in person, online, or following up after an interaction, every step helps you build a strong and supportive network. Here's how to put your skills to work and grow your connections.

Social Media and Online Networking

Social media isn't just for funny cat videos. It's a powerful tool to connect with people who share your interests or career goals. Platforms like LinkedIn, Instagram, or TikTok (for creative fields) can help you showcase your skills, meet mentors, and discover opportunities. Used wisely, social media can unlock doors you didn't even know existed.

Building a LinkedIn Profile

Think of your LinkedIn profile as your digital first impression. A strong profile helps you stand out and connect with people who share your interests or work in areas you want to explore.

Profile Photo: Your profile pic is key—make sure it's clear, professional, and reflects who you are. It doesn't have to be a formal headshot, but make sure you look approachable and put-together.

Headline: Your headline is like a mini elevator pitch. Keep it short and sweet, highlighting what you do or what you're passionate about. For example, "Aspiring Writer | Exploring Creative Careers" or "Future Software Engineer | Passionate About Problem-Solving."

About Section: This is your chance to share who you are and what excites you. Write in a friendly tone and let people know what drives you and what you're looking for. A personal touch makes you more relatable and approachable.

Connections: Start by connecting with people you know— family, friends, mentors. Then, branch out to those you meet at events, online communities, or through shared interests. Don't be shy about reaching out to people you admire; a friendly message can lead to great things.

Engagement: Stay active by posting updates about what you're up to, sharing thoughts, or commenting on others' posts. It's about building relationships and showing you're genuinely interested in what others are doing.

Role-Playing Networking Scenarios

Want to practice your networking skills? Try role-playing different scenarios to get more comfortable with making connections. Whether it's introducing yourself at an event or reaching out for advice, practicing helps you feel more confident and prepared.

Scenario 1: Meeting Someone New at an Event

• Formal: "Hi, I'm [Name]. I'm really into [topic] and noticed your work on [project]. Would love to hear more about your experience with it!"

• Casual: "Hey, I'm [Name]. I heard you're into [activity]—that's awesome! How did you get started?"

• Online: "Hi, I'm [Name]. I saw your post about [topic], and it really caught my attention. I'd love to hear more about your thoughts on it."

Practice these introductions with friends or family to feel more at ease when the real thing happens!

Scenario 2: Asking for Guidance or Mentorship

When you're reaching out for advice, it's all about being clear and showing that you're genuinely interested. Here's how to ask for mentorship or guidance in different settings:

- Formal Setting: "I really admire your work in [field]. I'm just starting out, and I'd love any advice or tips you might have to offer."
- Casual Setting: "Hey, I've always been curious about [field/topic]. What's one thing you wish you knew when you first got started?"

- Online: "Hi, I've been following your work in [field], and it's super inspiring! Do you have any tips for a beginner like me or resources you'd recommend?"

Tailoring your request to the situation makes it easier for people to respond and creates a more meaningful conversation.

Writing Follow-Up Emails or Messages

Following up is a great way to show you genuinely value the connection and want to keep it going. It also demonstrates professionalism and your desire to build something real: friendship, mentorship, or career connection.

Taking that extra step can really set you apart and help you develop lasting, meaningful relationships. Here are some email templates to get you started:

Thank-You Email:

"Hi [Name],

It was awesome meeting you at [event]! I really enjoyed chatting about [topic]. I'd love to stay in touch and learn more about your work in [field]. Let me know if you'd like to chat sometime!"

Request for Mentorship/Advice:

"Dear [Name],

It was such a pleasure connecting with you at [event]. I'm [Name], a high school student exploring [field], and I really appreciated your insights on [topic]. If you have the time, I'd love to follow up and hear more about your journey or any advice you'd have for someone just starting out.

Thanks so much for considering, and I hope we can stay in touch!"

Networking Challenges and Growth

Networking is a skill you get better at the more you practice. As you build and maintain connections, you'll find plenty of opportunities to push yourself and step outside your comfort zone.

Here are a few challenges to help you get started:

Challenge 1: Start Networking (No, seriously...like right now!)

Reach out to three people this month—maybe a teacher, a family friend, or someone you admire in your community. For example, ask your teacher for advice on a project, reconnect with a family friend who works in a field you're interested in, or introduce yourself to someone at a local event. These small, intentional steps can open up a ton of new opportunities and help you get comfortable networking. Starting with people you already know makes it easier to build confidence.

Challenge 2: Create a Networking Plan

Set both short- and long-term networking goals. A short-term goal could be attending one event a month or introducing yourself to a professional in a field you're curious about. A long-term goal might be building a mentoring relationship with someone you admire or expanding your LinkedIn network by 20 connections in the next six months. Breaking it down into small, actionable steps keeps you on track and helps you see your progress.

Challenge 3: Reflect on Progress

Taking time to reflect is key to improving. After each networking interaction, jot down your thoughts. Ask yourself:

- What went well? Did you make a good impression or ask interesting questions?
- What could you do better next time? Maybe be more confident or listen more attentively?
- Did you learn anything new or unexpected?
- How did the experience help you grow, both as a person and as a networker?

Keep a journal to track your growth over time. Celebrate your successes and reflect on any challenges—you'll be amazed at how much you improve!

Key Takeaways

- Networking is all about building genuine relationships that help everyone grow.
- Practice introductions to overcome shyness and focus on one-on-one connections.
- Social media tools like LinkedIn can help you connect with professionals, even as a teen.
- Always follow up to keep your connections engaged and the relationship going strong.

CREATIVITY AND PROBLEM-SOLVING

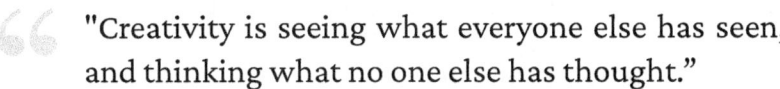

"Creativity is seeing what everyone else has seen, and thinking what no one else has thought."

— ALBERT EINSTEIN

C reativity and problem-solving are super handy skills that can help you crush it in all kinds of situations. You could be tackling a tough math problem, coming up with a killer idea for your school project, or figuring out how to use your free time in the best way possible; these skills are total game-changers. They help you tackle challenges and make life more fun, engaging, and fulfilling.

In this chapter, we'll dive into creativity and problem-solving, why they're a big deal, and how you can grow these skills to unlock your full potential and rock every area of your life.

Why Creativity is a Big Deal

Creativity is one of the most powerful tools you can have. It lets you look at challenges from fresh angles and makes even the most mundane tasks way more fun. Creativity helps you think outside the box and find extraordinary, unique solutions.

What Exactly is Creativity?

Creativity isn't just about being artsy, like drawing or playing music (though that's awesome, too!).

It's about using your imagination to approach problems or opportunities in new, interesting ways. It could be as simple as finding a clever way to organize your desk, writing a heartfelt letter to a friend, or figuring out a quicker way to get to school.

Creativity is everywhere, and it's what helps turn ordinary moments into something special.

Here are some everyday examples:

- Turning an old cardboard box into a fabulous storage solution for your room.
- Find a faster way to knock out your chores so you can relax and enjoy some free time.
- Coming up with a fun new game to play with your friends when it's rainy outside.

Creativity is what helps make life more fun, efficient, and exciting!

Benefits of Creativity

Now that we've got a good idea of what creativity is, let's take a look at all the incredible benefits it can bring to your life:

Helps You Solve Problems: When you think creatively, you can look at challenges in new ways and come up with solutions you might not have initially thought of.

For example, if you're stuck on a group project, creative thinking can help you suggest new approaches that simplify things or make them more exciting. It also teaches you to see problems as opportunities, leading to more creative and effective solutions.

It Lets You Express Yourself: Creativity is your chance to show the world who you *really* are. That could mean expression through writing, designing, or coming up with a clever solution to a problem; creativity lets you share your unique perspective and personality.

For example, you might design a fun flyer for a charity event to express your passion for helping others or write a short story that reflects your imagination and personal experiences. These creative acts help build your confidence and let others see the real you.

Boosts Confidence: Creating something new feels terrific! Every time you create, you build belief in yourself. That growing confidence makes you feel more ready to take on whatever comes next, knowing you've got the skills and creativity to succeed!

Keeps Life Fun: Trying new ideas and exploring different approaches keeps life exciting and full of variety. Experiment with a new recipe, freshly redecorate your room, or brainstorm a unique concept for a group project!

All of these little acts of creativity make life way more enjoyable and meaningful, adding adventure to even the most routine tasks.

Builds Adaptability: Creativity helps you think on your feet and adjust to whatever life throws at you.

For example, if the venue for a school event changes at the last minute, a creative mindset lets you:

- Brainstorm new locations.
- Adjust the schedule.
- Find ways to make the new space work just as well.

This kind of flexibility helps you face challenges with confidence and stay calm under pressure, turning surprises into chances for growth and success.

Problem-Solving Skills: Your Secret Weapon for Handling Life's Curveballs

Problem-solving is one of those skills that can totally change the game when it comes to handling life's challenges.

Let's say you are fixing a mistake, dealing with a disagreement, or figuring out the best way to spend your time; strong problem-solving skills can make everything smoother and more successful.

What Makes a Great Problem-Solver?

Being a top-notch problem-solver isn't just about fixing stuff—it's about understanding challenges on a deeper level and tackling them with a clear and strategic approach. Good problem-solvers can analyze a situation, adapt to new twists and turns, and think creatively to find solutions.

Here are some traits that make them stand out:

Critical Thinking: This is all about really understanding the problem by breaking it down and asking the right questions.

Instead of jumping to conclusions, an incredible problem-solver digs deep to discover why something is happening.

They might ask, "What's causing this?" or "What's the bigger picture here?" This kind of thinking helps you get to the root cause of the issue, so you're not just fixing the surface problem.

Resourcefulness: Sometimes, solving a problem means getting creative with the resources you've got!

Resourceful people know how to make the most of what they have available—using online resources to teach themselves something new, asking a teacher for advice, or teaming up with a friend to solve a tricky problem together.

If you're working on a school project but don't have all the materials, a resourceful person might repurpose stuff around the house or brainstorm new ideas to make it work.

Being adaptable and thinking outside the box is key!

Persistence: Not every problem gets solved instantly, and persistence keeps you going when the going gets tough. Even if you hit a roadblock, staying committed and pushing through challenges sets successful problem-solvers apart.

For example, getting stuck is part of the process if you're learning something new—like coding, playing an instrument, or mastering a tricky math concept. But you'll eventually crack the code by sticking with it and trying different approaches.

Persistence is all about not giving up, no matter how tough things get.

How These Skills Will Help You in the Future

At Work: Whether you're brainstorming creative ideas to improve things at work, fixing unexpected problems, or collaborating with others to meet goals, strong problem-solving skills make you stand out as a reliable, go-to team player.

Imagine this: you've got a deadline, and your main tool just broke down. With your problem-solving skills, you'd quickly find another way to get the job done, whether using a backup resource or getting creative with your approach.

Being able to solve problems on the fly keeps everything running smoothly and makes you the kind of person people want to work with.

In Life: As you grow, problem-solving skills become even more important for handling life's adult responsibilities. Managing a budget, planning a family trip, or even organizing your time requires thoughtful decision-making and planning.

For example, managing your money involves deciding how to:

- Save
- Spend
- Prioritize

When planning a trip, you'll need to think about everything from schedules to budget-friendly options while dealing with unexpected changes (like a delayed flight or a last-minute cancellation).

In relationships, whether with coworkers, friends, or family, listening and finding fair solutions to disagreements is key to keeping things smooth.

Problem-solving will help you stay calm, focused, and efficient as you navigate the complexities of adult life. So, by developing these skills now, you're setting yourself up for success later on!

Steps to Solve Problems

Identify the Problem: First things first—figure out what exactly needs fixing! As the old saying goes, "A problem well stated is a problem half solved."

So take a moment to ask yourself, "What's really going on here?" and "Why is this happening?"

Breaking it down into smaller chunks can make it feel less like a monster and more like something you can totally tackle.

For example, if you're running late on a project, is it because:

- Your time management is off,
- Roles are unclear,
- Are resources missing?

Once you pinpoint the root cause, you'll know exactly where to focus your energy.

Brainstorm Solutions: Now it's time to get your creative juices flowing! Jot down all the ideas that come to mind—even the weird ones. This isn't the time to judge your thoughts; it's the time to let your imagination roam free.

For example, if you want to make your study space more productive, maybe you can reorganize your desk or get fancy and build shelves from old cardboard boxes. The goal here is to come up with as many ideas as possible so you have plenty of options to choose from.

Evaluate Options: Once you have your list, it's time to play the "pro vs. con" game. Take a good look at each option and think about how realistic, efficient, or practical each idea really is.

For instance, if you're trying to save up for a vacation, should you cut back on Netflix and dining out or take on a side hustle?

Weighing the pros and cons helps you pick the one that hits the sweet spot between your goals and what you're willing to work with.

Take Action: Now for the fun part—actually doing something about it! Pick your solution and put it into play. If you decide to get a part-time job to save for that vacation, start applying to places or set up a gig online.

But, while you're at it, stay flexible. Sometimes, things don't go exactly as planned, and that's cool! Being able to pivot if needed will help you stay on track, even if bumps show up.

Reflect on the Outcome: After your solution's been in action for a while, take a step back and think about how it went.

- What worked?

- What didn't?
- What would you do differently next time?

Reflecting on the results helps you learn and improve, so you'll be even better prepared for the next challenge. For example, if you had to deal with project delays, think about how you handled it and how you can avoid the same hiccups next time. It's all about getting better and smarter each time!

What to do?	*How to do it?*
Identify the Problem	*Define, break it down, and find the root cause.*
Brainstorm Solutions	*Generate ideas without judgment.*
Evaluate Options	*Weigh the pros and cons and pick the best fit.*
Take Action	*Implement, stay flexible, and observe results.*
Reflect on the Outcome	*Review what worked and improve for next time.*

Table 9.1 *Summary of Problem-solving Steps*

How to Get Better at Creativity and Problem-Solving

Getting better at creativity and problem-solving takes time, but you can level up with the right mindset and a few tricks up your sleeve.

This section will walk you through some easy, practical steps to help you think outside the box and tackle problems like a pro, whether flying solo or as part of a team.

Building a Creative Mindset

Don't Fear Failure: Mistakes aren't the world's end—they're learning opportunities! Every time something goes wrong, consider it a lesson in disguise.

For instance, if you try to bake a cake and it comes out a little... off, figure out where it went wrong. Maybe the oven was too hot, or you missed a step?

Take what you learn and use it next time. Embrace those "oops" moments; they'll push you to get even more creative next time.

Stay Curious: Keep asking questions and diving into new things. Curiosity is like fuel for your creativity engine. If you come across something you don't understand, go ahead and look it up, explore it more, or even ask someone who knows.

Whether it's a new hobby like coding, photography, or learning about space—being curious helps you expand your mind and discover new ways to solve problems.

Think in Different Directions: Mix things up if the usual approach isn't working! Ask yourself, "Is there another way to tackle this?" or "What would someone else do?"

When you step out of your usual thinking patterns, you open up a whole world of possibilities. Rethinking your approach to a group project and shifting your perspective can spark fresh ideas and solutions that matter!

Be Open to Feedback: Creativity thrives when you let others in on the process. Share your ideas with friends, teachers, or family, and listen to their input.

You could be working on a school project, a piece of art, or a new story; feedback can offer new perspectives and make your work even better! Get into the habit of brainstorming with others—sometimes, the best ideas come when you least expect them!

Working With Others

Collaboration is key when it comes to creativity and solving problems—two heads (or more) are definitely better than one!

Working with others brings in new ideas and helps you see things you might have missed. Here's how teamwork can help you tackle challenges in the best way.

Teamwork Boosts Creativity

Working with a group can lead to breakthroughs that you might not get on your own. Everyone brings something different to the table, from new skills to fresh perspectives.

In a group project, for example, one person might be great at brainstorming ideas, while another excels at organizing.

Together, you'll create something better than any individual could alone!

Group Strategies

Brainstorming: This is where the magic happens—get everyone together and let the ideas flow! Create an environment where everyone feels comfortable giving suggestions, no matter how wild they seem. For example, in a community project, you might come up with ideas like bake sales, talent shows, or cleanup events. Once you have a bunch of ideas, you can narrow them down and choose the best fit.

Divide and Conquer

Let everyone play to their strengths by assigning tasks based on their skills. Does someone love designing? Let them handle visuals or presentations. Another person's great at organizing? They can keep track of the schedule.

By dividing responsibilities according to each person's strengths, the group works smarter, not harder.

Using Technology for Creativity

Technology can be a game-changer for boosting creativity and solving problems innovatively. With the right tools and apps, you can bring your ideas to life and collaborate more easily.

Here's how technology can take your creativity to the next level:

Apps and Tools

Platforms like Canva, Code.org, and Notion are fantastic resources for getting creative and staying organized.

- Canva lets you design cool graphics even if you're not a pro.
- Code.org helps you learn the basics of coding through fun projects
- Notion is great for keeping track of your ideas and tasks.

These tools are just a few examples—find what works best for you and start exploring. You'll be amazed at how these apps can boost your productivity and creativity.

Learn Online: There's no shortage of online resources to help you improve your creativity and problem-solving. You can find step-by-step tutorials on YouTube for pretty much anything, from graphic design to DIY crafts.

Online forums and virtual workshops also offer excellent opportunities to connect with like-minded people and experts in areas that interest you. The key is diving in, experimenting, and applying what you've learned to your projects.

Who knows what creative idea will pop up next?

Activities to Build Your Skills

Want to boost your creativity and problem-solving skills? The best way to do it is by having fun while practicing! Whether you're into hands-on activities or reflecting through journaling, these exercises will help you think outside the box, work with others, and get better at tackling problems in creative ways. Ready to jump in?

Creativity Challenges

Repurpose Everyday Items: Got an old jar lying around? Turn it into something amazing! You could paint it, wrap it in fabric, and voilà—it's a chic pencil holder or mini vase. Or, take a cardboard box and give it new life by turning it into a craft organizer, bookshelf, or storage bin.

The sky's the limit when you start thinking about how to repurpose the stuff you already have. It's a fun way to challenge your creativity—and you'll be helping the environment, too!

Try Creative Prompts: Sometimes, all you need is a fun prompt to spark your imagination.

Write a short story about what you'd do if you found a treasure buried in your backyard. What's the treasure? How did it get there? What happens next?

Or, get artsy and draw something inspired by nature—think leaves, rocks, flowers, and more. These little exercises are perfect for getting your creative juices flowing in unexpected ways!

Problem-Solving Scenarios

Real-Life Role-Playing:

Pretend you're in a real-life scenario that requires problem-solving.

For example, plan a surprise birthday party on a tight budget. First, figure out the problem: How do you create an unforget-table celebration without breaking the bank? Then, brainstorm ideas like DIY decorations or hosting the party at a free outdoor park.

Next, evaluate which ideas work best and take action! When it's all done, reflect on what worked and what you could do better next time. These exercises give you practice in problem-solving, adaptability, and planning.

Group Challenges

Teamwork makes the dream work! Try a group challenge like building a bridge out of popsicle sticks, solving an escape room puzzle, or brainstorming ideas for a new gadget. These tasks are perfect for sparking creativity, promoting collaboration, and learning to combine different perspectives to find the best solution. Plus, they're a lot of fun!

Innovation Projects

Create Something Useful

Why not create something practical and innovative? You could design a portable charging kit for all your devices or come up with a gadget that solves a common problem in your life.

Innovation projects like this help you think practically while still letting your creativity shine!

Reflective Journaling

Write About Your Experiences

It's helpful to reflect on challenges after they've passed. Try journaling about a recent problem you solved—describe the issue, how you figured it out, and what steps you took to find a solution.

Think about what worked and what you could have done differently. This reflection will help you sharpen your problem-solving skills for the future.

Track Your Growth

Keep a journal where you document your creative projects and problem-solving efforts. Over time, you can look back and see how much you've improved. It's an excellent way to celebrate your progress and stay motivated!

By practicing these activities, you'll be ready to take on challenges confidently and creatively. With each new task, you'll get better at turning obstacles into opportunities and have a blast doing it!

Key Takeaways

- Creativity helps you think outside the box and express yourself, while problem-solving helps you tackle challenges effectively.
- These skills build your confidence, adaptability, and ability to handle challenging situations.
- Tools like mind mapping, teamwork, and technology make developing these skills easier and more fun.
- Activities like journaling, creative challenges, and group projects are great ways to practice and grow.

Growing and Succeeding Together

THROUGHOUT THIS BOOK, we've explored essential life skills from time management and communication to financial literacy and decision-making. My hope is that these insights have equipped you with the tools and confidence to navigate challenges and take charge of your future.

As an author, nothing is more rewarding than hearing from readers like you. If you found this book helpful, I would greatly appreciate it if you could take a moment to leave a review. Your feedback not only helps me improve but also guides other teens in their journey toward personal growth.

Thank you!

CONCLUSION

Well, my friend, here we are at the finish line of our life skills journey! Or wait—is it the starting line? Plot twist: it's both! That's the beautiful thing about personal growth—every ending is just a fresh beginning in disguise.

Let's take a moment to celebrate this journey we've shared! We've navigated the captivating landscape of emotional intelligence with all its twists, turns, and occasional unexpected detours (like that road trip where the GPS suddenly decides you should explore rural backroads you never knew existed).

Remember when we first unpacked the five key components of emotional intelligence? Self-awareness, self-regulation, motivation, empathy, and social skills—our reliable companions throughout this journey!

These aren't just buzzwords to impress people; they're your secret ingredients for cultivating better relationships, reducing stress, enhancing mental health, and achieving career success without sacrificing your other life goals.

The emotionally intelligent version of you notices when you're feeling grumpy before you accidentally send that passive-aggressive email. This part of you understands why your class-mate or coworker might be having a rough day, knows how to stay motivated when social media calls your name and can navigate social situations without that internal voice scream-ing, "What do I do with my hands?!"

And then there's creative thinking—not just for those who wear berets and discuss existentialism over espresso! We discovered that creativity is your brain's way of throwing a surprise party, inviting different ideas to mingle and form unexpected friendships.

It's how we:

- Solve problems
- Find workarounds
- Sometimes, invent something amazing

Combining creative thinking with emotional intelligence gives you superpowers to maintain self-control and stay motivated, even when life throws curveballs at you.

Remember our pep talk about challenging yourself? Every time you try something new, your brain does a little happy dance and forges new connections.

That nervousness before doing something outside your comfort zone isn't your body saying, "Retreat!" Your internal growth meter says, "Ooh, expansion is happening here!" The next time you feel butterflies in your stomach, thank them for confirming that you're leveling up in the game of life!

Communication skills serve as the vital connection between your thoughts and the outside world. We've explored how different communication approaches work. Sometimes, you need the structure of assertive communication for important negotiations, while other situations call for the warmth of empathetic listening when supporting friends through difficult times.

Effective communication creates benefits beyond simple information exchange—it strengthens relationships, resolves conflict efficiently, and attracts new opportunities in both personal and professional spheres.

Our chapter on adaptability and resilience uncovered that flexibility isn't just for yoga enthusiasts! Your emotional insurance is your capacity to bend without breaking when life throws those inevitable curveballs.

And resilience—that magical bounce-back quality—turns out to be less like an inborn superpower and more like a muscle you can strengthen by tackling the weights of challenges. Each time you think, "Well, that didn't go as planned, but I'm still standing," you're becoming emotionally stronger!

Our technological adventure resembled exploring a digital jungle with the right survival tools! Being tech-savvy doesn't mean you have to code the next social media platform before breakfast—it's about confidently navigating online spaces instead of being confused.

Creating passwords that aren't "password123" (I see you!), understanding when AI is helpful versus when it's merely trying to sell you something, and knowing when to put the phone down and engage with actual humans with faces. It's about making technology work for you rather than feeling like you work for it!

Financial literacy might seem as thrilling as watching paint dry, but we've turned it into your money adventure game! Understanding your budget isn't about limiting joy—crafting a treasure map to discover more of it.

Learning investment strategies isn't just for those who look sharp in suits on Wall Street; it's about making your money work as hard as you do. When your finances are in order, you're not just wealthier in dollars—you're wealthier in choices, opportunities, and freedom.

Future You is already sending thank-you notes for the wise decisions Present You is making!

Time management—the eternal battle between what we want to do and the clock that stubbornly refuses to add extra hours!

We've learned techniques like:

- Time blocking
- SMART goals
- Pomodoro method

As we've learned, these methods aren't about cramming more productivity into every second. They're about making room for what truly matters while giving procrastination a friendly yet firm farewell.

Working smarter instead of harder means achieving more with

less exhaustion—leaving energy for the fun stuff! After all, life is too short to spend it all on your to-do list.

And for the big finish, networking—that word that makes many of us want to hide under the covers! We reframed it from "awkward social exchanges" to "making genuine human connections with people you enjoy."

Overcoming shyness, building confidence, and connecting authentically in the real world isn't about becoming someone you're not—it's sharing the wonderful person you already are with a world that could use your unique perspective and talents.

Here's the magical part: all these skills are interconnected like the most fascinating connect-the-dots puzzle in the world! Emotional intelligence helps you communicate better, making networking less daunting. Time management creates room for learning new skills, while financial literacy equips you with resources to seize opportunities. They are like the Avengers of personal development—each strong on their own but unbeatable when they unite!

As you finish this book and return to your regularly scheduled life, take a moment to give yourself a high-five (go ahead; I'll wait). You've absorbed knowledge that has the potential to transform how you navigate the world and experience it from within.

The beauty of this journey is that there are no final exams, no need for perfection, and certainly no comparison charts with others. Your only competition is yesterday's version of yourself. Even when you feel like you've taken a step backward, remember that learning isn't linear—sometimes, the path to growth includes loops, spirals, and the occasional scenic detour.

Start small! Perhaps it's practicing emotional awareness for five minutes daily, trying out a new budgeting app, or conversing with that interesting person at school instead of just thinking about it. Small, consistent actions act like compound interest for personal development—modest beginnings yield remarkable results over time.

The world is changing faster than ever, but you're now equipped with adaptable skills that will never go out of style. While specific techniques may evolve (remember when people used to store contacts in actual paper address books?), the core principles we've explored are timeless human operating systems.

So here's my challenge to you: Take these pages and turn them into action. It is not a perfect action, not a massive overnight transformation, but a curious, playful, step-by-step action! Be the scientist of your life, experimenting with these ideas and discovering what works for YOUR unique brain, personality, and circumstances.

The most important thing to remember is that you're perfectly imperfect, gloriously unfinished, and where you need to be on your journey.

And whenever you feel stuck or uncertain, remember: you've got this! Not because you'll always know exactly what to do but because you now have the tools to figure it out along the way.

Your adventure is just beginning—and it's going to be amazing!

NEXT STEPS

Throughout this book, we've explored many valuable skills and gained a wealth of knowledge. But the journey doesn't stop here! There's always room to grow and refine your skills even further. The books listed below are a great starting point for continued learning. You can find them on Amazon or search for the titles online to get started!

Financial Literacy for Young Adults Simplified
Discover How to Manage, Save, and Invest Money to Build a Secure & Independent Future

If you're new to personal finance, this book is the perfect starting point. It breaks down budgeting, saving, and investing into simple, actionable steps, helping you build a solid financial foundation and prepare for more advanced concepts ahead.

Financial Literacy for Young Adults Amplified
Prepare for Inflation & Recession, Decide Between Buying or Renting, & Borrow Smarter

This book explores advanced financial topics such as inflation and recessions, equipping you with the knowledge to make informed decisions—whether it's choosing to buy or rent or borrowing responsibly. It's a valuable guide to navigating real-world financial challenges with confidence.

Stock Investing for Young Adults Simplified
Discover How to Evaluate Stocks, Manage Risks, & Build a Winning Investment Strategy

Ready to dive deeper into investing? This book is the perfect next step, covering everything from stock analysis and risk management to crafting a strong investment strategy. It provides the essential tools to elevate your investing knowledge and make informed financial decisions.

Smart Money Habits for Young Adults to Build Wealth
Avoid Emotional Spending, Impulsive Investments, & Biased Thinking to Build a Secure Financial Future

This book explores how emotions and biases shape financial decisions and offers practical strategies to recognize and overcome them, leading to smarter money management.

REFERENCES

A Guide To Emotions | Psychology Tools. (2024, June 11). Psychology Tools. https://www.psychologytools.com/self-help/a-guide-to-emotions

Bailin, S., Case, R., Coombs, J. R., & Daniels, L. B. (1999). Common misconceptions of critical thinking. *Journal of Curriculum Studies, 31*(3), 269–283. https://doi.org/10.1080/002202799183124

Bdc. (2020, September 12). *Why communication is key to success.* BDC.ca. https://www.bdc.ca/en/articles-tools/entrepreneurial-skills/become-better-communicator/why-communication-key-success

Bentley University. (2018, October 19). *How technology is boosting your creativity | Bentley University.* Bentley University. https://www.bentley.edu/news/how-technology-boosting-your-creativity

Better Explained. (2019). *Understanding the Pareto Principle (The 80/20 Rule) – BetterExplained.* Betterexplained.com. https://betterexplained.com/articles/understanding-the-pareto-principle-the-8020-rule/

Big Future. (2025). *Networking Basics for High School Students – BigFuture.* Bigfuture.collegeboard.org. https://bigfuture.collegeboard.org/explore-careers/get-started/career-prep-high-school/networking-basics-for-high-school-students

Blackledge, J. T., & Hayes, S. C. (2001). Emotion regulation in acceptance and commitment therapy. *Journal of Clinical Psychology, 57*(2), 243–255. https://doi.org/10.1002/1097-4679(200102)57:2%3C243::aid-jclp9%3E3.0.co;2-x

Bokari, D. (2021, April 20). 5 Ways to Stop Procrastinating. *Boise State University.* https://www.boisestate.edu/coen-mbe/2021/04/20/5-ways-to-stop-procrastinating/

Boogaard, K. (2023, December 26). *How to write SMART goals.* Atlassian. https://www.atlassian.com/blog/productivity/how-to-write-smart-goals

Boyles, M. (2022, February 1). *What Is Creative Problem-Solving & Why Is It Important?* Business Insights Blog. https://online.hbs.edu/blog/post/what-is-creative-problem-solving

Brigden, B. (2024). *Leadership & Teamwork: 10 Ways Leaders Can Help Their Teams.* Www.teamwork.com. https://www.teamwork.com/blog/10-ways-leaders-teams/

Buzanko, C. (2023, October 24). *Empowering Young Minds: Developing Critical*

References

Thinking Skills in Children and Teens - Koru Family Psychology. Korupsycholo-gy.ca. https://korupsychology.ca/developing-critical-thinking-skills/

Cirillo, F. (2024). *Time Management Course - Pomodoro® Technique.* Www.po-modorotechnique.com. https://www.pomodorotechnique.com/

Crowley, L. (2019, February 13). *What are the three types of communication?* BeSpoke. https://bespoke-coaching.com/blog/what-are-the-three-types-of-communication/

Dealing with Feelings - The Mental Health Coalition. (2024, December 12). The Mental Health Coalition. https://www.thementalhealthcoalition.org/how-to-deal-with-emotions/?gad_source=1&gclid=CjOKCQiAkoe9BhDYARIsAH85cDM7kJFJcuCCYepBfc3AvfHFfeDuLvtAj8xEHHqozeXN6042g8qujcQaAlBdEALw_wcB

DePaul, K. (2022, May 10). *If Networking Makes You Anxious, Try This.* Harvard Business Review. https://hbr.org/2022/05/if-networking-makes-you-anxious-try-this

Dr. Ruth Gotian. (2021, December 28). 10 Ways To Boost Your Emotional Intelligence. *Forbes.* https://www.forbes.com/sites/ruthgotian/2021/12/28/10-ways-to-boost-your-emotional-intelligence/

Dweck, Dr. Carol. (2017). *Decades of scientific research that started a growth mindset revolution.* Mindsetworks.com. https://www.mindsetworks.com/science/

Eisenhower. (2011). *The Eisenhower Matrix.* Eisenhower. https://www.eisenhower.me/eisenhower-matrix/

Emerson, M. S. (2021, August 30). *8 Ways You Can Improve Your Communication Skills.* Professional Development | Harvard DCE. https://professional.dce.harvard.edu/blog/8-ways-you-can-improve-your-communication-skills/

Fidelity Viewpoints. (2024, June 3). *How to teach teens about investing | teens and money | Fidelity.* Www.fidelity.com. https://www.fidelity.com/learning-center/personal-finance/teach-teens-investing

Fox, S. (2024, May 4). *11 Essential Life Skills for Teens to Learn Now.* The SPARK Mentoring Program. https://sparkcurriculum.org/essential-life-skills-for-teens/

Gallo, C. (2022, November 23). *How Great Leaders Communicate.* Harvard Business Review. https://hbr.org/2022/11/how-great-leaders-communicate

Goldman, A. (2022, June 2). *What is an ETF? A Beginner's Guide | Wealthsimple.* Wealthsimple.com. https://www.wealthsimple.com/en-ca/learn/what-is-etf?utm_source=google&utm_medium=performance&campaign_id=13082057005&adgroup_id=120301247737&ad_id=600369036378&keyword=&gad_source=1&gclid=CjwKCAiAiOa9BhBqEiwABCdG86l

References

EEw1y55cq-jH6pRLWT1-
_EwCH9uHYylGh5H0BrFscmx4PTz5D7hoCbvAQAvD_BwE

Gormley Jr., W. T. (2017, November 29). *5 Myths About Critical Thinking*. FutureEd; FutureEd. https://www.future-ed.org/5-myths-about-critical-thinking/

Harvard Professional Development. (2019). *How to improve your emotional intelligence*. Professional Development | Harvard DCE; President and Fellows of Harvard College. https://professional.dce.harvard.edu/blog/how-to-improve-your-emotional-intelligence/

Hornbuckle, M. (2022, November 28). *YouScience National Survey Finds That Most High School Graduates Do Not Feel Prepared for College and Career Decisions*. YouScience. https://www.youscience.com/resources/press/post-graduation-readiness-report-press-release

ICAEW Insights. (2021, April 28). *The 5 Elements of Emotional Intelligence*. Www.icaew.com. https://www.icaew.com/insights/student-insights/student-insights-2021-archive/the-5-elements-of-emotional-intelligence

Jabaker. (2023, July 24). *Critical Thinking & Why It's So Important*. Nichols College. https://graduate.nichols.edu/blog/why-is-critical-thinking-important/

Koenig, J. (2019). *The Dictionary of Obscure Sorrows*. Tumblr. http://www.dictionaryofobscuresorrows.com

Martin, R. (2022, January 12). *50 tips for improving your emotional intelligence*. RocheMartin. https://www.rochemartin.com/blog/50-tips-improving-emotional-intelligence

Mayo Clinic Staff. (2023, November 21). *Positive thinking: Stop negative self-talk to reduce stress*. Mayo Clinic. https://www.mayoclinic.org/healthy-lifestyle/stress-management/in-depth/positive-thinking/art-20043950

Modu, E. (2025, January 2). *Stocks for Kids [2023]*. TeenVestor. https://www.teenvestor.com/stocks-for-kids

Mosunic, PhD, RD, MBA, Dr. C. (2023). *Here's why emotional intelligence is so important*. Calm Blog. https://www.calm.com/blog/why-is-emotional-intelligence-important

Motion Blog. (2023, June). *Eat the Frog: How to Take Control of Your Time & Get More Done*. Usemotion.com. https://www.usemotion.com/blog/eat-the-frog

Nyabeze, C. (2021, November 24). *The Value of Networking As a Teen: 10 Ways to make meaningful connections with the right people*. Future North. https://futurenorth.ca/the-value-of-networking-as-a-teen-10-ways-to-make-meaningful-connections-with-the-right-people/

Oregon.gov. (n.d.). *Division of Financial Regulation : Creating a personal budget : Manage your finances : State of Oregon*. Dfr.oregon.gov. https://dfr.oregon. gov/financial/manage/Pages/budget.aspx

Pascual, P. (2022, November 29). *14 Simple Rules That Will Make You A Better Communicator | Talaera*. Talaera. https://www.talaera.com/blog/14-simple-rules-that-will-make-you-a-better-communicator

Program, E. (n.d.). *Common Misconceptions and Partial Understandings Common misconception and/or partial understanding Extending our understanding of critical thinking*. Retrieved February 11, 2025, from https://www.edu.gov.mb. ca/k12/framework/docs/misconceptions_critical_thinking.pdf

Reboot. (2020, June 9). *Parents' Guide to Critical Thinking: Ages 13+ | REBOOT FOUNDATION*. Https://Reboot-Foundation.org. https://reboot-foundation. org/parent-guide/ages-13-plus/

Reitkopp, M. (2024, November 2). *Importance of Decision Making with a Dusting of Critical Thinking*. Medium. https://medium.com/@melissareitkopp/ importance-of-decision-making-with-a-dusting-of-critical-thinking-305a7c43dc7f

Segal, Ph.D., J., Smith, M.A., M., & Robinson, L. (2018, November 3). *Emotional Intelligence Toolkit - HelpGuide.org*. HelpGuide.org. https://www.helpguide. org/mental-health/wellbeing/emotional-intelligence-toolkit

Segal, J. (2024, September 25). *Body Language and Nonverbal Communication*. HelpGuide.org. https://www.helpguide.org/relationships/communication/ nonverbal-communication

Segal, J., Smith, M., & Robinson, L. (2024, August 21). *Improving Emotional Intelligence (EQ): Expert Guide*. HelpGuide.org. https://www.helpguide.org/ mental-health/wellbeing/emotional-intelligence-eq

Smart, J. (2020, February 11). *35 problem solving techniques and activities to create effective solutions*. SessionLab. https://www.sessionlab.com/blog/problem-solving-techniques/

Sonqishe, L. E. (2023, November 7). *Mastering The Art Of Critical Thinking: 7 Powerful Strategies*. Hypnotherapy Cape Town| Mindset Coaching | Lungisa Sonqishe. https://www.lungisasonqishe.com/mastering-the-art-of-criti cal-thinking/

Soots, L. (2016, December 29). *Communication is Key*. The Positive Psychology People. https://www.thepositivepsychologypeople.com/communication-is-key/

The Speaker Lab. (2024, August 31). *The Ultimate Guide to Public Speaking: 8 Tips and Techniques to Know*. The Speaker Lab. https://thespeakerlab.com/blog/ public-speaking/

References

The University of Tennessee. (2025). *Critical Thinking and Problem-Solving | University of Tennessee at Chattanooga.* Www.utc.edu. https://www.utc.edu/academic-affairs/walker-center-for-teaching-and-learning/teaching-resources/pedagogical-strategies-and-techniques/ct-ps

Types of savings | Savings Strategies - HSBC Bank USA. (2025). Hsbc.com. https://www.us.hsbc.com/financial-wellness/types-of-savings/

U.S. Department of Labor. (n.d.). *Problem Solving and Critical Thinking.* https://www.dol.gov/sites/dolgov/files/odep/topics/youth/softskills/problem.pdf

University of Saskatchewan. (2023). *Research Guides: Critical Thinking Tutorial: Interpreting Information Methodically.* Usask.ca. https://libguides.usask.ca/CriticalThinkingTutorial/InterpretingInformationMethodically

University, W. (2022). *how-to-be-an-effective-communicator-in-7-easy-steps.* Www.waldenu.edu. https://www.waldenu.edu/programs/communication/resource/how-to-be-an-effective-communicator-in-7-easy-steps

Western University. (2025). *Critical Thinking.* Teaching.uwo.ca. https://teaching.uwo.ca/teaching/learning/critical-thinking.html

What are the most effective ways to use body language and voice to persuade and influence others? (n.d.). Www.linkedin.com. https://www.linkedin.com/advice/3/what-most-effective-ways-use-body-language-voice

What is hands-on learning? (n.d.). Skillable. https://www.skillable.com/resources/hands-on-learning/what-is-hands-on-learning/

Whiteside, E. (2022, September 17). *What is the 50/20/30 budget rule?* Investopedia. https://www.investopedia.com/ask/answers/022916/what-502030-budget-rule.asp

Why Emotional Intelligence Matters Today More Than Ever. (2020, April 16). Action Strategies by Design. https://www.action-strategies.com/why-eq-matters-today-more-than-ever/

Wooll, M. (2022, March 14). *6 Important critical thinking skills you should master.* Betterup. https://www.betterup.com/blog/critical-thinking-skills

www.ingramcontent.com/pod-product-compliance
Lightning Source LLC
Chambersburg PA
CBHW071401120626
46546CB00002B/769